W9-BIS-903

The Industrial Revolution in Scotland

New Studies in Economic and Social History

Edited for the Economic History Society by
Michael Sanderson
University of East Anglia, Norwich

This series, specially commissioned by the Economic History Society, provides a guide to the current interpretations of the key themes of economic and social history in which advances have recently been made or in which there has been significant debate.

In recent times economic and social history has been one of the most flourishing areas of historical study. This has mirrored the increasing relevance of the economic and social sciences both in a student's choice of career and in forming a society at large more aware of the importance of these issues in their everyday lives. Moreover specialist interests in business, agricultural and welfare history, for example, have themselves burgeoned and there has been an increased interest in the economic development of the wider world. Stimulating as these scholarly developments have been for the specialist, the rapid advance of the subject and the quantity of new publications make it difficult for the reader to gain an overview of particular topics, let alone the whole field.

New Studies in Economic and Social History is intended for students and their teachers. It is designed to introduce them to fresh topics and to enable them to keep abreast of recent writing and debates. All the books in the series are written by a recognised authority in the subject, and the arguments and issues are set out in a critical but unpartisan fashion. The aim of the series is to survey the current state of scholarship, rather than to provide a set of prepackaged conclusions.

The series has been edited since its inception in 1968 by Professors M. W. Flinn, T. C. Smout and L. A. Clarkson, and is currently edited by Dr Michael Sanderson. From 1968 it was published by Macmillan as *Studies in Economic History*, and after 1974 as *Studies in Economic and Social History*. From 1995 *New Studies in Economic and Social History* is being published on behalf of the Economic History Society by Cambridge University Press. This new series includes some of the titles previously published by Macmillan as well as new titles, and reflects the ongoing development throughout the world of this rich seam of history.

For a full list of titles in print, please see the end of the book.

The Industrial Revolution
in Scotland

Prepared for the Economic History Society by

Christopher A. Whatley
University of Dundee

CAMBRIDGE
UNIVERSITY PRESS

HC
257
54
W47
1997

Published by the Press Syndicate of the University of Cambridge
The Pitt Building, Trumpington Street, Cambridge CB2 1RP
40 West 20th Street, New York, NY 10011-4211, USA
10 Stamford Road, Oakleigh, Melbourne 3166, Australia

First published 1997

Printed in Great Britain at the University Press, Cambridge

A catalogue record for this book is available from the British Library

Library of Congress cataloguing in publication data

ISBN 0 521 57228 2 hardback
ISBN 0 521 57643 1 paperback

CE

Contents

Acknowledgements

Professors Christopher Smout and Roy Campbell encouraged me to accept the challenge of writing this short book. My colleague Bob Harris has willingly read first drafts of the chapters and commented upon them from the perspective of the non-Scottish historian. His probing questions and sound advice have been invaluable. The series editor, Michael Sanderson, has been patient, considerate and enormously helpful. Mrs Helen Carmichael has assisted me in preparing the text for the publisher. Carolyn Bain of the University of Dundee's Media Services unit drew the map. That Shetland has been left off the map is not due to cartographic error, but results from the need to represent the Scottish mainland on a scale that is useful to readers. H. A. Whatley kindly compiled the index. Pat, my partner, has kept my spirits up when I was flagging, and deserves considerable credit for ensuring that I completed the task.

References

References are to numbered items in the bibliography e.g. [96]. Page numbers where necessary are italicised e.g. [96: *35*].

Map of Scotland

Introduction

Numerous books and articles have been published on the 'British' Industrial Revolution. Most however either ignore Scotland, or pay lip-service to it. In many cases there is a failure to recognise that generalisations, particularly of the macro-economic variety, about the nature, timing and causes of 'British' (i.e. what is in effect English) industrialisation do not necessarily apply to Scotland [153]. Often too, references to Scotland stress a single aspect – most frequently the cotton industry of Glasgow, Paisley and elsewhere in west-central Scotland, or the same region's coal and iron and related industries, which underpinned Scotland's 'Victorian economic miracle'. Important as this region and these products undoubtedly were to Scotland's economy, such approaches fail to recognise the diversity of Scotland's economic experience in the eighteenth and early nineteenth centuries. Keith Wrightson's observation that there were 'many Englands' is equally applicable to Scotland where there were several other identifiable economic regions [318:258]. Considerable attention will be paid in this book to the most important of these.

Outside the central Lowlands, the most distinctive region throughout the period was the Scottish Highlands and Islands, which accounted for some 20 per cent of the Scottish population in 1801, 350,000 people in 1831. There is much substance in the remark that Scotland in the 1840s was a 'dual economy', with the south becoming increasingly capitalistic and industrialised, whereas the north, which too had felt the impact of capitalist impulses, 'was a world of traditional values, oriented round the peasant desire to cling to a holding of land despite intolerable demographic pressures' [192:81].

In neither region however was the pattern of economic and social change uniform. Lowland Scotland was not simply a producer of cotton, minerals and ships. By the mid-nineteenth century the economy of Dundee and the towns and villages of the surrounding area in east-central Scotland had become firmly based on coarse linen and jute. In Dundee itself, Scotland's third town after Glasgow and Edinburgh, were located the world's two biggest mill and factory complexes, in linen and jute respectively [291]. To the south, in Fife, specialisation occurred in smaller towns such as Dunfermline, with fine linens. Manufacturing in the rural counties to the south of Edinburgh – Border country – was focussed on wool. Edinburgh itself had a sizeable textile industry which in 1841 was still the city's biggest employer of industrial workers, although reflecting the city's status as an educational, legal and cultural centre and the impact of its professional middle-class expenditure patterns it boasted Scotland's greatest concentrations of consumer industries and of those employed in food, drink and tobacco [247]. Aberdeenshire, the second county in Scotland in terms of population in 1755, had followed a pattern of economic development in the eighteenth century similar to the other counties of eastern Scotland, as hand-based manufacturing spread into the countryside. Yet while textile production had become concentrated in the regional centre of Aberdeen from *c*.1779, its virtual collapse between 1848 and 1852 heralded the emergence of a much more balanced economic structure than that of the 'one industry' town of Dundee [112; 286]. Although Aberdeen's distance from the coal and iron mines of central Scotland meant that it suffered from comparative disadvantages as far as steam shipbuilding was concerned, at least half a dozen firms concentrated on wooden vessels. Innovative and producing high-quality schooners, barques and clippers, the products of three firms were sought in increasing numbers by English purchasers in the 1830s and 1840s [106]. Aberdeenshire, on the other hand, became increasingly dependent upon agriculture after 1811, when rural employment in textiles reached its peak [287:*80*].

Meaningful analysis of industrialisation and its impact in such areas however requires even further spacial disaggregation by region and even sub-region: eastern Aberdeenshire, for example, was Highland, while the Lowland part of the county can be distinguished by two land types, recognition of which is crucial for an understanding of the product-base of proto-industry in the eighteenth century [287:*73–8*]. Similarly, conditions in the Highlands and Islands varied. The west highland coast and the islands of the Hebrides were measurably less well developed and poorer than the central, south-western and eastern highlands, where proximity to the industrial areas was one factor which determined the economic viability of both landed estates and sub-tenant household economies, largely through the operation of demand for products – such as slates from Argyll – and migrant labour respectively [31; 192:*10*; 202:*24*]. The effects of the Industrial Revolution were felt in the Highlands and Islands directly as well as indirectly. Even in west-central Scotland, which incorporated the counties of Ayrshire, Dunbartonshire, Lanarkshire and Renfrewshire, there was a massive contrast between the industrial powerhouse of Glasgow, the country's largest urban unit with a rapidly growing population which had reached 345,000 in 1851 (i.e. over one in ten Scots), and to the south, the rural villages and relatively small farms of Ayrshire outside the mining districts, which concentrated on beef production, and increasingly, dairying [36].

There are a number of reasons why Scotland should have figured less prominently than England in older accounts of the British Industrial Revolution. One is the parochialism of many English historians and the difficulties they have in incorporating Scottish material [182]. More important perhaps is that there has been nothing like the same wealth of usable statistical material which has been available to English economic historians, especially for the eighteenth century [209:*xi*; 31]. Sometimes the data simply do not exist. In other cases the time-consuming tasks of collation and manipulation have not been carried out. Partly as a result of this, but also because Scottish historians, economic and otherwise, have been and still are relatively few in number and thinly spread across a range of research topics, published work on the Industrial Revolution in Scotland as such has not been thick on the ground. Indeed the only book of any note with the phrase 'Industrial Revolution' in its title was first published as long ago as 1932 [143].

This is not to suggest that economic historians in Scotland have neglected the subject. Economic histories have been written and considerable progress has been made, in terms of sectoral, industrial and regional studies. Business historians, industrial archaeologists, social historians, historical geographers and demographers have all contributed to the deepening pool of knowledge. From the later 1970s Scottish economic and social historians began to engage in comparative analysis. This has borne most fruit where Scottish and Irish economic and social history has been concerned, although comparisons with Scandinavia have also been revealing, as have attempts to place Scottish demographic patterns within a European framework [61; 90; 162; 214]. Thus examination of landownership patterns in Denmark, where peasant proprietorship was increasingly common after *c.*1780, points to the importance for Scottish modernisation of the power and passion for agrarian progress of Scottish landowners in a society in which land proprietorship was confined to 2 per cent of the population, a much lower figure than for Norway for instance [273; 274].

It might be objected that there was no distinctively *Scottish* Industrial Revolution, and some historians have correctly observed that the industrialisation process of which it was part was a wider British and European phenomenon. From 1603 Scotland and England had shared the same monarch. Incorporating union had followed in 1707. Political and cultural links had been forged prior to this, most visibly between Lowland Scotland and the four northern counties of England, where there were several shared social characteristics [157:*16–17*, 262–4; 116]. Trade, overland and coastwise, with England was substantial, and undoubtedly contributed to the processes of economic growth and industrialisation. Scotland gained enormously from the legal right which she had post-1707 to trade with and exploit in other ways England's expanding colonial empire, itself a component part of the emergent European world-economy. As will be seen, English capital flowed northwards, as did English technology and expertise. An example of the merging of the English and Scottish economies is the Borders woollen industry, which after 1707 'became integrated more closely with the economy of the north of England than with that of Scotland itself', with large quantities of Scottish wool being transported to the West Riding of Yorkshire, and Scots in the southern counties being recruited as outworkers by English worsted manufacturers [140:*36*]. On the other hand, Scotland made important contributions to England's – Britain's – Industrial Revolution [23]. This is most notable in the sciences and civil and mechanical engineering. Men such as Charles Macintosh, the founder of Manchester's rubber industry, Charles Tennant, of St Rollox bleachworks, the Fairbairn brothers, renowned engineers in Leeds and Manchester, James Watt and Thomas Telford and others, were Scots who had benefited either directly or indirectly from the uniquely rational methods of enquiry taught by the Scottish universities in the eighteenth century [34:*34–7*].

Yet there is a case for treating Scotland separately. Although a stateless nation after 1707, Scotland was in many respects a distinctive political, economic and social entity [37; 213]. Scotland's economic fortunes were a crucial issue at the time of the Union, and even after 1707 certain specific Scottish economic interests were discussed and legislated upon at Westminster. The Union preserved several uniquely Scottish institutions, such as the legal and educational systems and the Church of Scotland. These, some economic historians contend, made real contributions to the Scottish economy in the eighteenth century. The influential Board of Trustees of Manufactures, established in 1727, was a specifically Scottish body, and an influential one at that, and other quasi-state agencies also served to further the economic ambitions of a self-consciously patriotic professional and business elite. As will be seen in what follows, it can be argued that in terms of the timing, nature and causes of her Industrial Revolution, Scotland was sufficiently different to justify separate treatment. Such a study will make for a deeper understanding of Britain's industrialisation process.

The time is now ripe for a survey and synthesis of the literature referred to above. For one thing, the long-running debate about the British Industrial Revolution is currently in the midst of one of its more active phases. Secondly, there has recently been a resurgence of interest in the idea of the Industrial Revolution as a regional and local phenomenon [163]. Concerns about the limitations of national accounts and aggregate statistics as a means of identifying and understanding the Industrial Revolution, and the recognition of marked regional disparities, have led some economic historians to conclude that 'regional studies may be of more value in understanding the process of industrialisation than studies of the national economy as a whole' [6:*38*]. Thirdly, there is now just about sufficient published material available on the Scottish economy in the seventeenth, eighteenth and nineteenth centuries to make it possible to identify and provide a fresh explanation for Scotland's Industrial Revolution, and to offer a Scottish contribution to the ongoing debate about the characteristics and explanations for the Industrial Revolution in Britain. Much more work remains to be done however, as will become apparent from this study.

It will have been noted that the terms 'Industrial Revolution' and 'industrialisation' have been used above interchangeably, with no attempt having been made either to define or to distinguish between them. This is not the place to become embroiled in the debate about the adequacy of the concept of an 'Industrial Revolution' [216; 226]. Clearly, it has many drawbacks, not the least of which is the confusion over its precise meaning, which can vary from historian to historian [152]. Rondo Cameron and others have argued that contemporaries seemed unaware that they were living through such a cataclysmic event, although to include Scots such as Robert Burns and Sir Walter Scott amongst those who might have been expected to have commented upon it, but did not, is to overlook the former's fascination with and visit to Carron ironworks and the latter's terror of the growing grumblings of the working classes [26]. And while it is certainly the case that no Scottish contemporary used the term 'Industrial Revolution', there can be no denying that many of the clerical contributors to the parish-by-parish statistical accounts in the 1790s were acutely aware that major change had begun and that manufacturing and industry was on the march [102:*44*].

The received view amongst Scottish economic historians is that Scotland did experience an Industrial Revolution, and that this started later and was more compressed than its English counterpart [104:*97–9*]. As should become apparent later, this is because whatever doubts there may be about the applicability of the term 'Industrial Revolution' to England, arguably, there are fewer in Scotland's case.

There is however considerable uncertainty about its precise timing and characteristics, due in part to the absence of any substantial attempt on the part of those concerned to define their terms. Various starting dates have been proposed: the 1740s, 1760s and 1780s (the most common) [31], and even 1830 [94]. The last follows the late Professor H. Hamilton who argued for a two-stage process: the first, led by cotton, beginning in 1780, and a second, commencing in the 1830s and lasting until *c*.1880, in which iron, engineering and shipbuilding were predominant [143:*1*].

Nevertheless, following gradualist interpretations of the English Industrial Revolution, there are those who have been inclined to question the notion of sharp turning points [199:*161–2*; 189:*101–2, 155*]. That the process of industrialisation was incomplete by 1830 would be accepted without reservation [192:*10*]. Campbell has recently drawn attention to the continuing dominance of the landowner in a Scotland which in 1830 'was still a rural country' [37:*93*]. Rapid and profound structural change however was under way, and whilst recognising such continuities, others argue that a 'major and decisive break with the past' had occurred, and that between 1780 and 1840 Scotland had become 'irreversibly, a different kind of society' [81:*60–61*; 266; 189:*155*]. This was certainly the case by 1850, the concluding date for this volume. Both symbolic of and contributing to the new order was the railway, which played a crucial role not as a consumer of the products of Scotland's emerging heavy industries but rather in opening up the coal deposits of central Scotland [288]. Before the mania of 1845–46 the new lines had been essentially of local importance, but by mid-century they had linked the main towns of Lowland Scotland. Significantly, the border with England had been crossed at two points.

What will immediately strike the reader who is familiar with the debates about economic growth, 'modernisation' and industrialisation in England is the relative absence in the Scottish case of series of sophisticated statistical data in the form of estimates of national income, per capita income, total factor productivity and occupational structure. Measures of this sort have been crucial to recent interpretations of the English economy in the eighteenth and early nineteenth centuries [55; 175]. Other important building blocks upon which discussion of England's eighteenth century economy and Industrial Revolution have rested, such as the analysis of the social structure of England and Wales in 1688 by Gregory King, have no – or only partial – Scottish equivalents prior to the 1790s, when the invaluable *Statistical Accounts* of all of Scotland's parishes were compiled under the direction of Sir John Sinclair. Heroic attempts however have been made to analyse Scottish social structure in the 1690s from surviving poll-tax data from which a firmer impression of the nature of the pre-industrialised economy can be obtained [313; 157; 82].

The next two chapters seek to provide from the available published evidence an outline description of the key features of and developments in the Scottish economy from the later seventeenth century until around 1850. At the same time, attention will be paid to the wider historiographical context and some consideration given to how Scotland's experience accords with current interpretations of the 'British' Industrial Revolution. Thereafter the reasons for Scotland's Industrial Revolution will be discussed, and then followed by a chapter which concentrates on social aspects and consequences. Throughout, heed has been taken of the series editor's plea that, above all, the book should 'let us [non-Scots] know what actually happened in Scotland'. For those readers who wish to know more, an extensive but far from exhaustive list of references, which also acts as a bibliography, has been keyed into the text.

1
Identifying Scotland's Industrial Revolution (1): the pre-Union inheritance

The search for an Industrial Revolution in England has been made more difficult with the appearance of a strong body of national economic data which shows that economic growth took place over a longer time-span and with less sharp breaks and more modest structural change than earlier accounts had suggested [55]. As a consequence, greater emphasis has been placed on the early modern period, and in particular the seventeenth and early eighteenth centuries [44]. Around 1700, it has recently been argued, England was ' "prepared" for an industrial revolution' [226].

Characterisations of the Scottish economy in the seventeenth century have changed markedly over time. Traditionally, it was portrayed as both poverty-stricken and peripheral, and in relation to England and much of northern Europe, a 'byword for ... backwardness'. Even though attempts were made to improve matters after the Restoration, one historian has concluded that at no point between the mid-sixteenth century and the early eighteenth 'did any important change occur' [183:*48*].

Such dismal portrayals of Scotland's pre-Union economy are certainly not without foundation, although it should be noted that one reason for them has been the anxiety of pro-unionist historians to point to the advantages which were brought by the Union of 1707 [276]. Over the past three decades however a much more positive view has emerged, to the extent that the roots of later eighteenth-century advance have been traced back to the previous century. This revised perception has two main components: first, that Scotland's economy and society was much more dynamic and conducive to economic growth than was formerly assumed, and secondly, while there was much about Scotland which was distinctive, in several important respects the country was similar both to England and other more advanced parts of northern Europe, 'the Sweden of the British Isles' [60:*229*].

The heftiest revisionist blows have been struck in the critical agrarian sector. The notion of stasis was first undermined and then swept away with the uncovering of a substantial body of evidence showing that Scottish agriculture in the 1600s was becoming commercialised and responding to new market opportunities. In the second half of the seventeenth century, Scottish landowners in the fertile cereal-growing east had managed in many seasons to export grain. Within Scotland, new outlets were created by a 'dramatic' rise in the number of market centres after 1660. Although to what extent is not known, these reduced dependence upon subsistence farming and assisted too in drawing the High-lands into the market economy; by 1707 only 18 per cent of mainland Scotland was more than 20 km from such a centre, 246 of which were created between 1660 and 1707 [307:*185*]. The numbers of black cattle driven south from the Highlands and western islands rose from the early 1600s, as did quantities of herring, salmon, timber, and skins and hides [130:*77–8*]. Grain was sent from Orkney to Norway, amongst other places, while Shetland fish were bought by German and other merchants [252]. Commercialisation is also reflected in the process of commuting rents in kind to money payments, albeit slowly. Greater efficiencies were sought through a reduction in the numbers of multiple tenancies and a rise in the use of longer, written leases [307]. Indeed there was a greater degree of stratification amongst the tenantry in rural Lowland Scotland than has sometimes been supposed [313]. Steps were taken too to extend the area of cultivation, by draining mosses and burning turf, and to improve yields and bring into cultivation former waste lands, by liming and manuring, which had begun in the sixteenth century, and were well-known in some regions by the mid-seventeenth.

Nor was the urban sector static, although owing to difficulties in interpreting the evidence there is disagreement about both how it fared overall and the precise movements within the urban hier-archy. Undisputed however are the estimates of the populations of the larger European towns (10,000-plus) which show that Scot-land, like England, but unlike most of the rest of western Europe, experienced continuous growth after 1550. In fact this concerned only two Scottish towns, Edinburgh (*c.*35,000 inhabitants in 1691), and Glasgow (*c.*18,000) [197]. Traditionally, Scotland's economic strength had lain in the east, where trade links had been forged with Scandinavia, the Baltic and northern Europe. To some extent this is reflected in the fact that the country's five most densely populated counties lay in the Forth basin [119:*188–9*]. New calculations based on hearth tax returns for 1691, and including small towns of 1,000 or fewer inhabitants, suggest levels of urbanisation in this region which matched those of the Netherlands [198:*35–6*].

Although Edinburgh only housed some 4.5 per cent of the Scottish population in the 1690s, and was therefore not as powerful an 'engine of growth' as London was in England, the Scottish capital (in population terms second only to London in Britain, and with a broadly similar socio-economic profile) was not only wealthier than its relative size indicates but also exercised a considerable pull on the surrounding countryside [96:*165*; 160]. It is notable that the most agriculturally improved area in Scotland was the Lothians although demand for foodstuffs from Edinburgh was felt more widely than this, with the grain-growing estates of Strathmore in Angus being just one of a number of east coast regions which were pulled into the orbit of the capital from the 1660s [132]. That the combined population of the other four largest towns, Glasgow, Aberdeen, Dundee and Perth, was twice that of Edinburgh and 'exceeded that of the capital to a greater degree than in most other European countries' was also economically important, although to what precise degree remains to be ascertained [310:*28*]. It may be that by exerting favourable pressures on employment and wages such towns contributed to the creation of the more homogeneous economy which has been observed in contrast to that of Ireland, where the greater gulf between high real wage rates in Dublin (higher than in Scotland in the later 1600s) and low rates for the unskilled in the countryside may be indicative of relative underdevelopment [62:*104–16*; 60:*239*].

Yet some caution has to be exercised when assessing the extent of urban expansion and the speed of change. It has been argued that many of the second and third rank provincial centres – towns such as, respectively, Aberdeen and Dundee, and Ayr and Dumfries – were no more populous in 1691 than they had been in 1639, and in many cases may have been less [198:*31*]. Growth appears to have taken place lower down the urban hierarchy (in towns of less than 2,500), notably in some of the newer burghs of barony (fifty-one of which were founded between 1660 and 1707), but not exclusively in these. (Burghs of barony were established from the later medieval period, under royal charters granted to individual barons. Unlike the royal burghs, economic activities were confined – formally at least – to the territory of the burgh itself; in this respect however the difference between the two was much less in practice than in theory [1].) As in England, small towns within the economic orbits of major centres like either Edinburgh or Glasgow appear to have done better, as did market centres within regions experiencing economic growth; other successes were marketing towns in the richer agricultural areas such as Angus, and a handful of places which were emerging as specialist industrial centres. Thus functional specialisation clearly existed within the Scottish urban hierarchy [309; 198:*33*].

Industrial change and expansion had occurred in several directions. Most important was the emergence of flax and linen as a leading sector in the Scottish economy. Long scattered throughout the country, mainly for local consumption, the commercial linen trade was by the early 1700s largely concentrated in five counties, Angus, Perthshire and Fife in the east, and Lanarkshire and Renfrewshire in the west, with most organisation, financing and marketing being carried out by urban merchants based in the monopolistic royal burghs [311:*232*]. Woollen production (of cloth – such as plaiding and 'fingrams', a coarse serge made from combed wool – and hosiery) had also become concentrated, notably in Aberdeenshire, where both trades were in the hands of Aberdeen-based putting-out merchants who then exported the bulk of the produce [287:*66–8*]. Growth occurred too in the extractive industries, especially in coal mining but also in lead, which began to be smelted in Scotland [148:*68*; 265]. New industries such as glass and more important, paper making, were established, albeit on a small scale [279].

Development and change can be discerned too in the organisation of production, not only in the extension of the putting-out operations of urban merchants, but also in their involvement in the establishment of large manufactures, a high proportion of which were in towns. As many as 106 of these may have been either proposed or established between 1587 and 1707, with almost three-quarters of them appearing (in the records at least) after 1660 [203]. Scotland too, it has been claimed, could boast a handful of collieries which ranked alongside the largest in Britain [148:*109*]. Organised (as far as can be ascertained) along rational capitalist lines, the manufactures are one indication, and indeed a partial result, of the growing determination of the Scottish state, acting upon mercantilist principles, to refashion the economy. Beginning in the early 1600s, but with greater coherence after the Restoration, the Scottish Privy Council and Parliament passed a series of general and specific acts which were designed to tackle structural weaknesses such as capital shortages, low-grade raw materials, acute shortages of skilled labour, and competition from abroad, and to stimulate and protect Scottish-based enterprise [203:*130–3*; 34:*17–19*]. The measures also included statutes devised to encourage agrarian reform [311:*94–112*].

The broadly positive role in economic development post *c.*1660 of the Scottish landowners has long been established [264]. Attention however has also been drawn to the active part played by the urban merchants in the larger Scottish towns, as well as – in Edinburgh – to the equally dynamic contribution to economic change made by factions within the craft guilds [160:*351–9*]. Edinburgh professionals such as surgeons and lawyers were also remarkably active investors in the main colonial, manufacturing and banking enterprises in late seventeenth-century Scotland [96:*100–6*]. Merchants' sons however formed the largest single category of new entrants to the urban business class. Far from being a static caste, the ranks of the merchant guildry were constantly refreshed by new blood by the end of the seventeenth century. Much of this came in the form of the sons of the landed classes, encouraged by the desire to improve their financial standing in the case of the first-born, and by the legal tradition of primogeniture where younger sons were concerned, who often aspired to purchase land on their own account, as did numbers of the more successful, socially aspiring merchants [69:*35–7*]. Scottish society at this level then was ambitious and fairly fluid (and in this respect not unlike England). What is more, such men had often obtained a sound commercial education, and through kinship links and personal contacts both within Scotland and in London, were able to establish both short- and long-term credit networks using 'novel' financial devices such as bills of exchange [69].

As has been suggested, important changes occurred in the composition of Scottish trade over the course of the seventeenth century. Scottish landed and mercantile opportunism had long been in evidence [142:*67*; 295:*34–9*]. More significant however was that whereas at the end of the sixteenth century Scottish exports had been overwhelmingly (but not exclusively) of raw materials and foodstuffs – primarily hides and skins, fish, wool and coal – a century later linen manufacturing, mainly in and around Glasgow, topped the list [142; 263:*237*]. Substantial quantities of both yarn and cloth went to England, and accounted for as much as two-thirds of Scottish exports to the south in some years, and never less than a third. Black cattle formed the other important component of the south-bound export stream [317]. The direction of trade saw some shifts too, although the Scottish pattern, which was largely interwoven with established links with the Low Countries, France and Scandinavia and the Baltic, remained broadly the same until the later 1600s, when Scotland's involvement in England's wars and economic nationalism began to cut into these linkages. The most significant new departure was the opening, in defiance of the English Navigation Acts, of the transatlantic routes to the West Indies and North America, sources of sugar and tobacco; small numbers of small Scottish ships too sailed to Ireland and further afield to Iberia.

Clearly, Scotland's economy was by no means as backward as was once assumed, and to this catalogue of achievement can be added other factors which support a more optimistic assessment of Scotland's economic strengths at the end of the seventeenth century. Probably the most important is population mobility: large numbers of Scots were prepared to move, more often temporarily, but also permanently, in search of employment, an apprenticeship, higher living standards, or for marriage [312].

What is equally clear however is that despite the similarities there were with England, the real progress which had been made, and the potential for growth which has been highlighted by recent comparisons with Ireland, Scotland was considerably less developed and also poorer and weaker than her southern neighbour [61]. In the crucial agrarian sector for example enclosures and instances of tree-planting beyond the policies of the landowners and gentry were rare. Cottars on the other hand were still to be found in substantial numbers in the majority of Lowland parishes for which poll tax data for the 1690s have recently been analysed. Even though the agrarian sector was normally able to feed the non-urban population, beyond the Lothians and the south-eastern Borders most Scottish farming was concerned with 'scarcity and survival rather than surplus and profit' [97:*272*]. In many parts of the Lowlands a peasant social structure still prevailed, unlike England where until recently the received view had been that peasant farming and attitudes had virtually disappeared – if not universally [319:*45*; 82:*11–16, 167–93*]. Advances in agriculture tended to occur within the existing rural social framework, where 'the forces of continuity were more powerful than the forces of change' [82:*16*]. Such a judgement can be applied with much greater force in the Highlands, even while recognising that older depictions of the pre-Clearance era as one of unimproved barbarity will no longer suffice. Sales of black cattle were drawing Highlanders into the commercial economy of the south [201; 243:*44–5*].

Scotland then was still overwhelmingly rural, 'a peripheral, marginal, largely upland country with a mainly pastoral economy'; almost nine out of ten Scots in an estimated population of just over 1.2 million in 1691 lived in a countryside which was characterised by dispersed farmsteads, cottages and hamlet clusters with few nucleated villages [311:*230*]. England's urban population was 18.7 per cent in 1700. As Scotland was much poorer domestic demand was also weak, although less so on the part of the elite who sought high-quality and luxury goods, which, by and large, were imported. The economy was also subject to short-term fluctuations [131:*167–71*]. Wage levels for the unskilled were lower in Scotland than in England, and, unlike English rates, failed to rise post-1650. Enterprise was thereby inhibited. Although estimates of mortality rates during the 'ill years' of the 1690s vary, and there were marked regional variations, the indications are that it may not have been until around 1740 that the population was restored to its pre-1690s level [119:*164–86*; 285].

There were some similarities in the Scottish and English financial systems, with the innovative Bank of Scotland being established in 1695, one year after the Bank of England, and there are signs that bills of exchange and informal credit networks may have existed earlier and to a greater degree and lower down the social scale than has been suspected hitherto [45: *314*; 96]. Even so, coin was chronically scarce, and the reported buoyancy of savings levels in England was not replicated north of the border [205:*131–2*]. Relative poverty is reflected in material culture too: although household size, structure and function in parts of the Lowlands were not unlike England, Scottish houses were smaller and less well furnished, while tenant farmers, for example, lacked household goods such as crockery and cutlery of the standard which was becoming commonplace in many parts of England [293:*60*].

With a minuscule navy to protect it, Scots shipping and therefore overseas trade, vital to the Scots, but of little importance to anyone else, was vulnerable in an age of muscular mercantilism [189:*48*; 297]. Contemporaries were acutely aware of this, more so after the Darien disaster than before. The failure of this ambitious venture by the Scots to create a trading colony in the Isthmus of Panama and the weaknesses of the Scottish economy it exposed was one factor which drove some Scots towards the incorporating union of 1707, with its promise of access to English markets and protection on the high seas. In the world context, pre-Union Scottish trade was 'trifling', and substantially less than England (the value of exports and re-exports was around one-fifth or one-sixth of the English level), Holland and France, 'or even Norway, Sweden and Hamburg' [263:*28–9*]. The value of Irish exports per capita was around 6s. at the end of the seventeenth century, while the Scottish figure stood at 4s. [61:*4*].

The existence of large manufactures such as Newmills should not detract attention from the small size and what appears to have been the underdeveloped nature of the commercial rural manufacturing sector: proto-industry was still in its infancy [308:*129*]. There were limits to the degree that changes in organisation and technology in urban manufacturing had occurred [160:*349*]. Further emphasising the distance which Scotland was from anything approaching an early Industrial Revolution is new research which has revised downwards previous output estimates for the linked industries of salt and coal. With output of coal from Scotland possibly as little as 225,000 tons, less than half Prof. J. U. Nef's figure, the claim that the industry was a 'major' growth element in the Scottish economy seems exaggerated. Exports of both coal and salt were minimal by the later 1600s [295:*40*, *146–7*].

Indeed almost without exception, the components of Scotland's small industrial sector were struggling by the turn of the eighteenth century, and would almost certainly have continued to do so even if markets had not been cut off by war and tariff barriers. At home demand was slight: annual per capita consumption of iron was roughly a quarter of England's 15 lbs [268:*605*]. Deep-seated weaknesses remained, mainly the poor quality of manufactures, a result in large part of a lack of a sufficiently large pool of indigenous technical and business know-how and a shortage of the appropriate labour skills, which often had to be imported from abroad at high cost. Thus in the case of woollen cloth, exports of which from Scotland were only 2 per cent of those of England at the end of the sixteenth century, decline had set in by the end of the 1600s. Newcomers to the industry such as Sweden – where labour costs were even lower – were easily able to compete with Scotland's coarse cloths [10; 141; 142; 287]. In the early eighteenth century, cattle were the largest single item of trade exported to England, which by then was Scotland's main external market [317:*157*].

In sum, there is much substance in the claim that the main lines of eighteenth-century development had been laid before the Union, and that Scotland was an economy and society of considerable potential. Much however remained to be achieved. The Scottish and English economies had been travelling in a similar direction, but England was many miles further down the road. The relative backwardness of the Scottish economy at the turn of the eighteenth century serves to strengthen the suggestion that her Industrial Revolution was indeed revolutionary: the more backward the economy, according to economists such as Alexander Gerschenkron, the more rapid will be the rate of industrialisation.

2

Identifying Scotland's Industrial Revolution (2): Union to *c.*1850

Although the immediate post-Union decades are something of a dark age in Scottish economic historiography, in Scotland there is less evidence of the general buoyancy which has been identified in the English economy over the period *c.*1685–1725 [293]. In some sectors of the domestic manufacturing economy the incorporating union was clearly damaging. Even though there were some short-term benefits which included soaring grain exports and a rise in the numbers of black cattle crossing the border, the failure of 1707 to bring sustained and widespread rewards forced even (hesitant) pro-Union contemporaries such as Sir John Clerk of Penicuik to concede that in most respects the Scottish economy *c.*1730 was much as it had been thirty years earlier [297].

Far too much emphasis however can be placed on 1707 as a turning point in Scottish economic history. Clearly it had an *effect*, but on its own it did not mark a substantial change in either the direction or the pace of Scottish economic life. The trends established earlier in the previous century were maintained, if uncertainly prior to the 1720s, as the Scots assessed and began to adjust to the new market situation. This was one of risks as well as opportunities within the British mercantilist framework [74:*28–9*].

Colonial links strengthened while modest improvement in the performance of the critical agrarian sector may be indicated by its capacity to feed the Lowland population – even during the crisis years of 1740–41. Although other important ameliorating factors played their part agrarian reform was occurring in the south-east Lowlands in particular. This took the form of more common use of longer, written leases, the strong but variable and incomplete move towards the payment of rents in money and consequent commercialisation of rural society, and a radical reduction in multiple tenancies [82]. Continuity as well as readjustment can be seen in the founding in 1723 of the Honourable Society of Improvers in Agriculture. In part this also represented the growing and widespread patriotic concern there was in influential circles about the condition of the Scottish economy in general and the linen, fishing and woollen industries in particular. This led in 1727 to the establishment of the Board of Trustees for Improving Fisheries and Manufactures, a body charged with the responsibility of raising the quality and output of these Scottish products [30:*51*]. The Royal Bank of Scotland was also founded in 1727, while in 1728 the cash credit system (a form of overdraft) was inaugurated [220:*3*; 254:*118–24*]. Growth across the board however is difficult to discern, although behind the economic cycles and severe downturns in 1725–26 and 1728, series of output data which are available are suggestive of modest if uncertain improvement in the domestic market in the first half of the eighteenth century [144:*301*; 219:*35*; 295:*44–56*].

Progress in an economy which contemporaries recognised was under-performing but rich in potential was represented by the appearance on the face of the countryside of a scattering of extractive and manufacturing enterprises. The Scottish-Irish coal trade, which had commenced in the early 1600s, experienced the first of its three eighteenth-century booms in the 1720s, much to the consternation of the Lowthers in Cumberland [294:*54–8*]. Many parts of the country, including the islands, were scoured for minerals by speculators such as Sir Archibald Grant of Monymusk [265; 63]. Hand frameknitting, introduced into Scotland by the state-supported Newmills Company in 1682, spread to Glasgow and the west in the 1740s [141:*12–14*]; coarse woollen cloth production survived the Union and expanded in some localities, usually where manufacturers were able to distinguish their products from those of England [140:*32–3*]. Paper making too saw further expansion, with new mills being opened, mainly in the vicinity of Edinburgh, still the country's most affluent centre, with its 'unequalled breadth and depth of legal, educational, religious, and governmental services' [160:*4*; 279:*118–24*]. All demanded paper.

For the first phase of Scottish industrialisation however, undoubtedly the most important developments were in flax spinning and the weaving of linen cloth. In the former, additional female hand spinners were recruited not only in the established spinning districts of central Scotland and the north-east, but during the 1730s and 1740s further north and into the Highlands. Demand for yarn, the quality of which was improved both by Board of Trustees supervision and more regular and closely monitored work, intensified within Scotland, as well as from England and Ireland. Weaving, hitherto performed badly and mostly customer work undertaken by weavers with little capital or credit, expanded too, with an extension of the putting-out system and an increase in the number of weaving sheds and factories. It was less successful (in the coarse end of the trade) than the yarn sector however and output of cloth approved and stamped by Board of Trustees stampmasters rose slowly from 1728 until the mid-1740s. By 1748–52 annual average output however was more than double the 1728–32 level [111].

Despite all this, in structural terms relatively little had changed by mid-century. Economic expansion tended to develop slowly and in accordance with an established pattern, with agriculture and rural society continuing to predominate. The reshaping of the Scottish Lowland countryside was limited (and even more so in the Highlands, the innovations of the second duke of Argyll notwithstanding), with rig cultivation (where heavy soil was ploughed into high broad ridges, from which water drained into furrows), and infield-outfield systems remaining commonplace. Agricultural productivity was low – perhaps half or less in oats – compared to England [57; 82:*42*]. Several of the more spectacular attempts at 'improvement' failed, or achieved little. A simple rise in the number of black cattle heading south (estimated to have risen from around 30,000–37,500 in 1723 to 40,000 *c.*1740) may have signified nothing more than an unchanged ranching economy in the Highlands, with the greater benefits – dung and the returns from droving and sales of fattened beasts – accruing elsewhere [270:*55–7*]. Manufacturing was still weakly established and burdened by restraints which had been evident in the seventeenth century. Linen, for instance, Scotland's 'staple', was in the coarse end of the trade heavily dependent upon export bounties [111:*65*]. While yarn spun in Scotland found a ready market in England and

Ireland, the weaving sector was dominated by small master-weavers who, as has been noted, were chronically under-capitalised and produced poor quality cloth which was much inferior to its Baltic rivals. Compared to its competitors, the Scottish bleaching industry had been 'lamentably deficient' in 1727, and made only slow progress thereafter [111:55].

After a post-Union surge the tobacco trade had stagnated after 1723 and up to *c*.1739, owing to a crack-down on the Scots merchants' customs chicanery, but perhaps more to their lack of capital resources at a time of low prices in Europe [241]. The spectacular progress made in coal mining in Ayrshire was not sustained after *c*.1730, while many of the Forth-side collieries (many of which were integrated coal and salt works) still depended on tax concessions obtained in 1707 to fend off competition from Tyneside in the home market, along with the revenue from sales from the protected salt industry [295]. Scottish trade with Ireland was slow growing and unstable, and declining in the case of imports up to *c*.1730 [49]. Technologically, Scotland was a long way behind the best practices of her nearest rivals. Hardly a single industry of any consequence outside the urban craft sector (building for example) was capable of expansion without the assistance of imported skilled workers [304:*24*; 305:*364*]. Those which attempted to compete with England or elsewhere beyond Scotland's shores found that they were confronted by problems of high production costs due to inefficient organisation and methods and the poor quality of their output. One consequence was a shortfall in manufactured goods from Scotland for the Chesapeake trade: Scottish tobacco merchants trading with Virginia and Maryland had to arrange for goods such as German linens and groceries to be shipped on account from London or other English ports.

The weakness of the Scottish manufacturing sector is well-exemplified by iron. Although charcoal-smelting in Scotland had first taken place in the early seventeenth century, the industry failed to secure a firm foothold anywhere, even after 1700 [15;193]. Similarly, coal output rose, but domestic demand was not sufficiently strong to encourage more than a handful of colliery proprietors to invest in Newcomen pumping engines [189:*63*].

Nevertheless, while no sharp turning point can be identified, during the 1740s and into the third quarter of the century, there was what can best be described as a quickening and widening of economic activity, suggesting that Scotland's growth pattern in the eighteenth century may have followed that identified by Deane and Cole in their study of British economic growth [67:*50–62*]. It was during the 1740s for example that the manufacture of 'Osnaburgs' began, in imitation of German linen from Osnabrück. Sales of this category of cloth rose at a 'spectacular' rate (from 0.5 million yards to 2.2 million yards between 1747 and 1758) [111:*27*; 301]. This was largely in the east: in the west, Paisley, following Glasgow, began to establish a reputation for fine threads and linens and lawns, and in 1759 silk gauze weaving was begun, and managed, with a substantial input of Spitalfields capital, to compete with London [196:*99*]. In wool, native enterprise tapped Board of Trustees expertise and funds to import superior English waulk (fulling) mill technology [253]. Another traditional product, 'uisge beatha' (whisky), which had mainly but not entirely been manufactured on a small but wide scale, saw the construction of a number of larger distilleries in the later 1740s and early 1750s [219:*35–6*].

Linen was employing as many as 20,000 handloom weavers in the 1760s, and at the very least, one female spinner from every second or third family [270:*64*]. Linen provided at least three-quarters of Scotland's textile exports, which in turn accounted for some 40–50 per cent of all Scotland's home-produced exports. As much as half of Scottish-made linen (overwhelmingly the coarse varieties, including Osnaburgs) was exported, either to England or abroad (notably to the colonies), as well as Ireland, where demand was particularly strong from the 1750s until the 1780s [111:*144–55*; 270:*64–5*; 49:*58–9*].

A model investigation of the strengthening Scottish economy in mid-century however emphasises the broad front upon which economic advance was occurring [270]. Even more striking than the steepening rise in the output and export of linen was the success of the re-export trade in tobacco. This was based on the credit-creating 'store system' operated by the tight-knit Glasgow merchant elite who through their factors purchased tobacco (preferably in return for goods rather than cash) directly from the farmers and bore the risk of selling it. The turn-round time of Scottish ships was thereby shortened. By the 1750s Glasgow was rivalling London. Just under half of Scottish imports, and in 1762

52 per cent of her exports, were of tobacco. The modern view is that the multiplier effects of the substantial investment of Glasgow and colonial merchants, not only in 'obvious' concerns such as sugar refineries where vertical integration occurred, but also in coal-bearing land, and a range of manufacturing enterprises, were of 'considerable' importance after *c*.1730 in the western Lowlands, the most dynamic region in Scotland. In some cases entire industries were dominated by colonial merchants – leather and boot and shoe making for example. In others, malleable ironworks, glassmaking (and to a lesser extent iron, linen and cotton), they played a major role. Even where they were less important numerically, merchant-backed firms could be of major pioneering importance [68:*38–40*]. Their indirect impact was felt at Carron Iron Works, opened in 1759 and often seen as a symbol of the advent of Scottish industrialisation, and which owed much to the demand from Glasgow merchants for its products [30:*47*]. They also promoted banks, specifically the Glasgow-based Ship, Arms and Thistle Banks, and thereby contributed to one of the fastest-growing sectors in mid-century, there being a fifteen-fold increase in banknotes between 1744 and 1772, when thirteen provincial banking companies opened their doors, thereby generating lines of credit in and around regional centres such as Aberdeen and Dundee. Bank assets rose from £329,000 to £3.1 million [270:*56*; 220].

Growth at this stage however was insecurely based: in 1762, balance of payments difficulties, the withdrawal of perhaps £500,000 of English capital, and retrenchment on the part of the Scottish banks, created crisis conditions [144:*305–13*; 45:*108–11*]. The Ayr Bank crashed spectacularly in 1772, and was partly responsible for bringing an end to the inflationary boom of the previous decade. The per capita value of home-produced goods in Scotland was probably still four or five times less than in England [270:*66*]. Linen was Scotland's only manufactured commodity of any importance, while a wide range of manufactures was imported from the south. Scotland's overseas trade was still conducted on a small scale, principally with Europe, and apart from Glasgow and her outports, which included the east coast port of Bo'ness, grew slowly in the 1750s, '60s and '70s, with only seven ports clearing more than 5,000 tons outwards in 1775 [170:*118–19*].

In terms of per capita exports however, Scotland was rapidly catching up with Ireland. Population began to rise from its mid-century level of some 1.3 million, having made good the losses of the 1690s, but much more striking was the pace of urban expansion, which in the second half of the eighteenth century was faster than virtually anywhere else in northern Europe [75]. Along with the growing numbers of industrial workers who were located in 'planned villages', the number of new foundations of which rose sharply during the 1760s and 1780s, urban expansion acted as a powerful 'engine of [economic] growth' [1:*64*]. In this respect Glasgow and Edinburgh, with the construction of its New Town from the 1760s, played crucial roles, with Glasgow replacing Edinburgh as the main focus of the metropolitan grain market in Scotland in the second half of the eighteenth century [132:*279*]. It is in the 1760s that historians have identified a sharp rise in demand for coal in Scotland [108:*23*], while it has recently been argued that it was from this period that major structural change and radical improvements in productivity occurred in Scottish agriculture, as the older but by no means rigid order was 'exposed to unprecedented and extraordinary market pressures' outlined above [82:*42*]. Other indices too point to a new era in Scottish economic history: rural day labourers' wages, which had remained virtually unchanged since the 1660s, began to rise in the 1760s, and to move closer to English levels; the differential in the wages of the unskilled and skilled in the building trades too was reduced in the Lowlands, and began to resemble the English pattern [131:*276, 279*].

Scotland's Industrial Revolution is most commonly held to have commenced at the end of the 1770s, with the appearance of cotton spinning mills at Penicuik in Midlothian and at Rothesay, Bute. As in Lancashire, the move into cotton production had not been without precedent [42:*11–16*]. As has been seen, Glasgow and Paisley merchants had long specialised in fine linens and had begun to make French cambrics and lawns [143:*91–2*]. Fustian manufacture was in evidence in 1730, and imports of raw cotton wool into the Clyde from the West Indies and the southern states of North America were not insubstantial before the first cotton cloth was woven in Scotland. Indeed it is important to recognise that, contrary to the long-held view that the Scottish cotton industry emerged as a result of capital being transferred from the tobacco trade after the interruption to it caused by the American War of Independence, the roots of the fine cotton industry in the west of Scotland lay in the flax, linen and silk trades. Attracted by the prospects of cloth sales from the growing demands of fashion-conscious middle- and working-class customers, but faced with rising labour and flax costs at a time when raw cotton prices were dropping, many linen merchants, including David Dale who was to become one of Scotland's leading cotton masters, were persuaded to spin fine cotton yarn with imported – sometimes pirated – English technology [18:*116–17*].

Reliable output figures for cotton do not exist. Measured by raw cotton imports, and numbers of mills and capital invested, however, growth was spectacular. From an annual average of 0.43 million pounds between 1781–86, imports of raw cotton rose five-fold by the end of the decade, and almost 17–fold, to 7.19 million pounds by 1799–1804. Estimates of the number of mills vary, but the most commonly reported figures suggest that in the nine years following the construction of the first cotton spinning mill in Penicuik in 1778, another 18 may have been opened; by 1795 there were some 39; 110 in 1810; by 1839, 192.

Initially, most of these were small and water-powered, although some were built to house hand-operated jennies [253:*320*]. As in England, cotton was at first an 'industry in the countryside', and in the 1780s and 1790s spinning mills opened as far south as Dumfriesshire and spread north through Stirlingshire, into Perth-shire, and Aberdeenshire in the north-east [253; 100:*23–8*]. There-after however, with the application of steam power from 1798 – later than in England – cotton spinning became increasingly concentrated in what had always been the industry's core region of Glasgow and Paisley. The Scottish industry however remained significantly more heavily dependent on water power than the north of England: in 1835 water accounted for 43.6 per cent of the Scottish industry's h.p., compared to the former's 18.6 per cent [42:*19*]. This was so even in the vicinity of Glasgow; in neigh-bouring Renfrewshire the River Cart basin provided much of the 41.5 per cent of the county's motive power which was derived from water in 1838 [253:*335*]. Whatever their principal power source however, the size of firms grew, with the credit crises during the

French Wars weeding out the smaller companies [18:*123*]. Fixed capital in spinning mills alone in 1812 was estimated at £1.4 million; by c.1840, with the tendency towards larger firms being firmly set, the total capital value of the whole industry, including finishing, was some £4.4 million.

Textiles lay at the heart of the first phase of Scotland's Industrial Revolution. According to Sir John Sinclair, between them, cotton, linen, wool and silk employed some 257,900 individuals in the early 1800s. This accounted for 89 per cent of all recorded manufacturing employment. The fastest rise was in mechanised spinning, but underlining the dual nature of employment in industrialisation, the number of handloom weavers rose too, from around 25,000 in 1780, to 78,000 thirty years later. The peak was reached around 1840, when over 84,500 people were employed on handlooms in Scotland [222:*23*]. Powerlooms however made rapid progress north of the border at first, and in 1813 more than half of those employed in cotton in Britain *may* have been located in Scotland [43:*113*]. Thereafter however, its adoption was 'fitful and slow', owing to its unsuitability for weaving fine cottons [223:*219*]. At the opposite end of the technological range were growing numbers of females who were engaged from the 1780s as embroiderers by muslin manufacturers who were based mainly in Glasgow and Paisley, although it should be noted that many workers had formerly been hand spinners. In 1851 the trade may have employed 25,000 individuals, mainly in the south of Scotland, although many more were employed – often by Glasgow firms – in northern Ireland [50].

Of those employed in textiles, around 60 per cent were in cotton, to which linen had lost its prime position by 1800, as in England it had superseded the centuries-old staple, woollen cloth. It is misleading however to suggest that Scotland's early Industrial Revolution was 'confined to cotton', although it is true that a town such as Paisley, which had traditionally concentrated on fine linen goods and, from the 1750s, silk gauzes, was forced to turn to cotton production (with the weaving of imitation Indian shawls from 1803 maintaining its reputation for quality work) [48:*10–13*]. What should not be overlooked is that linen output continued to expand, tripling in volume between 1773–77 and 1813–17 to an annual average of 26.6 million yards [111:*22*]. That its value only doubled over the same period (to £1.15 million per annum) underlines the fact that the industry was increasingly concentrated on coarser, lower-priced fabrics which were the speciality of the east coast county of Angus, where over half of all Scottish linen was being made by 1820. The country's three main linen producing counties, Angus, Fife and Perth, were making more than twice as much linen as the whole of Scotland had been in 1760, when Glasgow was Britain's premier linen town. Its west coast location meant that, already, cotton wool was proving to be a more appropriate raw material than Baltic and Russian flax [258:*85*; 173:*220*].

The introduction of English water-powered spinning technology from 1787 led to mills being built throughout the coarse textile area, and a consequent slow decline of hand spinning [284]. Following an uncertain start in steam-powered flax spinning in Dundee between *c.*1792 and 1818, the industry became increasingly concentrated in the port town and regional centre. Rapid growth followed, in the number of mills, the quantities of flax, hemp and later jute imported (there was an 11–fold increase between 1815–19 and 1845–49), in coastal shipments and in particular exports of linen cloth, which rose spectacularly, from 44 million yards in 1831 to 79 million in 1845 [174; 115].

In one sense all this is unexceptional. Similar developments were occurring in many parts of Britain. Significantly however, the regional concentration of industry has recently been characterised as one of the defining features of the Industrial Revolution. Thus despite the fact that the rate of growth of the linen industry remained roughly constant, the centralisation of production in Scotland on Dundee and its smaller satellite towns such as Forfar or Brechin, and the sub-regional centres of Dunfermline and Kirkcaldy, each with their own particular speciality, has much in common with rapidly industrialising regions south of the border such as the West Riding of Yorkshire [6; 65:*141*]. In terms of the speed of the adoption of mechanised forms of production, east central Scotland far outpaced Ireland, with which the Scottish industry had had much in common in the eighteenth century [115]. Within Scotland, Dundee's rise was ultimately at the expense of her previous northern rival, Aberdeen, where textile manufacturing was compensated for by diversification into fishing and meat processing, clipper construction, granite quarrying and, uniquely in Scotland, comb-making [112]. By 1826 Dundee had overtaken Hull as the UK's premier flax port, and was rivalling Leeds as Britain's principal linen producer. Not unlike Bradford, Dundee was transformed into an industrial town within the space of two or three decades, with a higher proportion of its workers employed in manufacturing (mainly textiles) than any of the other three large Scottish towns [247:*36–7*; 300].

Although on a considerably smaller scale, regional concentration also occurred in the woollen industry. The Border towns of Galashiels and Hawick became the main centres of Scottish woollen cloth and hosiery production respectively, along with the Hillfoots in central Scotland, with lesser centres in the south-west, and east Aberdeenshire. Unlike the former English woollen cloth producing regions of East Anglia and the west of England, the Scottish woollen industry did not decline at the expense of Yorkshire, but grew [165:*172*; 140:*38*].

Like linen, wool spinning and manufacturing had been scattered throughout much of Lowland Scotland, and parts of the Highlands and as far north as Shetland, in the central decades of the eighteenth century. In Aberdeenshire and the adjacent part of Kincardineshire alone, some 30,000 people, mainly women, had been employed part-time in hand-knitting stockings in 1795 [287:*68–71*]. Such mechanisation as had occurred before 1785 was largely confined to waulk (fulling) mills. By 1830 however, all processes apart from weaving and knitting were capable of being mechanised. The first mills to be built housed imported scribbling and carding machinery, although many also incorporated hand-powered spinning jennies, and were widely dispersed, at least outside the main cotton and linen producing districts. Although some concentration did occur, the creation of the locational pattern described above required the introduction in the 1810s of water- and steam-powered spinning, the last being essential for the post-*c.*1830 development of the industry in Stirling and Clackmannan, where suitable water supplies were limited. By 1835 ninety mills were in operation in Scotland, and 182 by 1850; the workforce almost tripled, to some 9,500, as the Scottish industry supplanted the West of England in the fine woollen trade [177:*80–2*]. From a position where Scotland had no woollen spinning mills (in 1790, when there were an estimated seventy-seven in the rest of Britain), the country's share had risen to an estimated 7.4 per cent of the total by 1830; over the same period fixed capital investment in mills alone may have risen from £3,000 to £170,000 [176].

The stocking-frame, small numbers of which had been used previously in many parts of Scotland, but especially the central belt (including Glasgow and Edinburgh) and the south-west, dealt a fatal blow to the low-cost country knitters of Aberdeenshire. This was in addition to that delivered by the French Wars from 1793, which had cut off formerly critical overseas markets. What is striking however is how rapidly framework knitting was established in the Borders, where it had been of little consequence until as late as the 1790s. By 1844 Scotland's 2,365 worsted frames, most of which were in the southern counties, 51 per cent in Hawick alone, were capable of producing around a quarter of Britain's woollen hosiery [141:*20–31*].

Textile finishing saw equally important developments, even though bleaching on a commercial scale had only been introduced into Scotland after 1727. The period of most rapid expansion was 1765–90, when over 100 new bleachfields were laid out. By the early 1800s there were between 200 and 250 bleachfields in operation, mainly in central and eastern Scotland, but also in more distant locations although a process of regional concentration had begun in the 1790s [253:*231*; 113]. Although most cost only a few hundred pounds to set up, several were major undertakings, requiring capital sums in the region of £4–5,000, owing to the high costs involved in levelling and irrigating large acreages of ground, of boiling and drying houses, machinery and equipment, housing and other buildings. By the 1790s, both organisationally and technologically, the best, such as those in the vicinity of Perth, were 'well able to stand comparison with any in Europe', and by the early 1800s were attracting cloth from both England and Ireland [113:*2*].

Increasingly, sulphuric acid was substituted for natural acids, after the establishment by Dr John Roebuck of a plant for manufacturing the product at Prestonpans in 1749, three years after a similar works had been set up in Birmingham [144:*140–1*], while in 1787 the much more rapid process of chlorine bleaching was introduced. With the establishment by Charles Tennant of St Rollox works in Glasgow in 1799 for manufacturing bleaching powder, Scotland became a world leader in chemicals, with St Rollox being the largest heavy chemical plant in Europe in the 1830s and 1840s [258:*133*]. Print and dyeworks were also established: Turkey red dyeing for example began in Glasgow in 1785, expanded there and gained a favourable Europe-wide reputation, but became concentrated in the Vale of Leven, with its purer water and clean air [278].

The emerging picture of rapid growth and profound change in the Scottish economy in the later decades of the eighteenth century becomes even clearer when the extractive industries are included. Traditionally, the Scottish coal industry in the eighteenth century has been associated with slow growth [33:*15*; 108:*32–8*]. New calculations however suggest that rather than rising four-fold, which is slower than the rate for Britain as a whole, there may have been as much as a ten-fold increase in output between 1700 and 1800, and a thirteen-fold increase if the period is extended to 1830. This is significantly faster than the national rate, although by no means as fast as those achieved by mining regions such as Lancashire, Wales and the South-West of England [303: *7*; 120:*26*]. Even so, on the basis of the new estimates, Scotland's share of British output rose between the 1690s and 1800, from some 8.1 per cent to 13.3 per cent, with a sharp upturn after *c.*1760. Both in terms of technical awareness and capital commitment, by 1800 Scotland had one of the best records amongst the British mining regions as far as the provision of steam pumping equipment was concerned [303:*15*].

Also growing rapidly in comparative terms was the paper industry, which like coal, lime and slates was also geared to the burgeoning home market. 'Phenomenal' growth occurred between 1779 and 1790 (although this may partly reflect new administrative procedures in the administration of the excise, returns from which provide the basis for the output data), while again between 1824 and 1852, after widespread mechanisation had taken place, the Scottish growth rate surpassed that of England, with Scotland's share of UK output rising from 10.7 to 22.2 per cent [279:*77*, *192*]. Rising consumer demand, from within Scotland but also from south of the border, stimulated a flurry of construction of legal whisky distilleries in Lowland Scotland in and immediately after 1779, and on an even greater scale following the Wash Act of 1784. These sizeable distilleries were at the heart of extensive networks of agricultural production and markets (for barley and rye for example) and included some of the largest manufacturing undertakings in Scotland in the 1780s. James Stein at Kilbagie boasted Scotland's first Boulton & Watt steam engine. Distilleries therefore made their mark, as yet unquantified, on Scottish coal output, although not in the Highlands where thousands of small, seasonal and largely illicit peat-fired stills flourished – allegedly supplying half the whisky consumed in Scotland – until they began to be suppressed from the early 1820s [219:*48–72*; 84:*118–34*]. The demand for whalebone stays, industry's need for oil and the effects of the American Revolution on the price of whale oil stimulated new-found interest in whaling in ports such as Aberdeen and Montrose [169]. All this – evidence of broad-based economic advance – supports the recently revived contention that there was a sharp rise in industrial activity in Britain after *c*.1780 [175].

Before 1830, iron played a relatively small part, with demand for coal from pig-iron producers accounting at that date for probably no more than 11 per cent of Scottish coal output; the UK equivalent was 18.6 per cent [120:*252–3*]. Scotland had only one 'leading sector'. The establishment of Carron marked a new expansionary phase in the Scottish industry's history, although it was not until 1779 that a second coke-using works was opened, at Wilsontown in Lanarkshire. The following two decades (until 1801) saw 'dramatic' expansion: no new works however was built thereafter in Scotland until 1824 [199:*190*]. Output rose, but only by 125 per cent between 1796 and 1830, a rate which was considerably slower than that for the UK as a whole [15; 145:*268–9*]. Scotland's iron industry suffered from several problems, but the most pressing was almost certainly an historically low level of domestic demand, which left it vulnerable to downturns in trade elsewhere [17]. Under-capitalisation prior to *c*.1830 was another problem. Like most iron-producing regions in Britain, the Scottish industry was sheltered from the low-cost Welsh industry by the cost of transportation, but even so Scotland's share of UK production appears to have been considerably reduced between 1788 and 1815 [168].

Data such as this appear to provide qualified support for a 'two-stage' concept of Scottish industrialisation after c.1780. Changes in the Salt Laws in 1825 led, belatedly, to the virtual collapse of the salt industry, by now an insignificant remnant of the 'old' pre-Union economy [295]. Kelp (seaweed) burning too suffered from the same legislation: burgeoning demand for the alkali it produced, from the soap and glass industries of the south, had taken the tentacles of industrialisation onto the shores of the far north and west coastline of Scotland after 1750. The price peaked around 1810 however, and after 1825 created increasing difficulties for the 50,000 or so people who were dependent upon earnings from it [136:*155–8*; 243:*132*]. Illicit whisky production too diminished sharply, as has been seen. The numbers of ships engaged in whaling at Aberdeen and Peterhead fell after 1821 and 1825 respectively, while there was a major cut-back in production from Scotland's emergent shipbuilding industry [208:*70*; 170]. After the boom of 1825 the cotton industry never again experienced its previous levels of buoyancy, and after a long period of stagnation, slowly followed its Irish counterpart downwards, as it ran up against overseas competitors which had emerged during the Napoleonic Wars, and slipped further behind Lancashire which was consolidating its technological and organisational superiority over the Scots [30:*106–9*; 93:*111*; 10]. In wool too, serious problems were encountered in the 1820s, with a fall in the quality of the wool from Cheviot sheep, and the unsuitability of Scottish plant and skills for dealing with the finer imported wools being used in Yorkshire. There was also an unwillingness on the part of many Scottish manufacturers to tackle the new threat head on, preferring instead to follow the easier course, producing cheaper, low-quality cloths [140:*64–9*]. After overcoming earlier shortfalls in supply, the west of Scotland coal industry periodically found itself with surplus coal, which was 'dumped' on the Irish market in the early 1800s in a bid to drive up Glasgow prices [49:*32*]. Even the early success of the Clyde steam shipbuilding industry, which had seen it seize 60 per cent of British output between 1812 and 1820, was checked, and reduced to 14 per cent of the total, in the following decade [258:*127*].

The case for a 'break' in the Scottish industrialisation process can be exaggerated however and may have been confused with what was a general period of slackness in the British economy which lasted from the collapse in 1825–26 until a new phase of prosperity commenced in 1832 [45:*409*]. Indeed in most sectors the upturn had begun long before this. Temporary if deep recessions apart, the textile economy of east central Scotland continued to expand throughout the first half of the nineteenth century. The challenges confronting the Borders woollen industry were more fundamental and required radical solutions, but even so the remarkable expansion of the productive capacity of the industry in the succeeding decades 'was rooted in the products of the pre-tweed era' [140:*70, 85*]. What 'changed' in the flax and linen towns of the east were production methods, principally the extension of the use of steam to drive mills and loom factories – which along with gas works and other urban users generated in Dundee a phenomenal five-fold increase in coal imports from the collieries of Fife and the Lothians (as well as Tyneside), which was shipped from expanding coal ports such as Alloa and Charleston on the Forth [174]. The early nineteenth century as a whole was a period of 'massive' port development along Scotland's east coast [188]. This was in line with the rest of Britain, where port capacity tripled between 1791 and 1841; and, as in England, a handful of ports (Glasgow, Aberdeen, Dundee, Leith and Bo'ness) increasingly dominated the country's seagoing trade [171:*98*]. Shipping figures for Glasgow, Port Glasgow and Greenock (with a fleet of 662 vessels, aggregating a remarkable 187,545 tons in 1841) show steady and significant improvement in the 1820s and 1830s, with cotton cloth, iron goods and other manufactures featuring prominently amongst the exports [173].

The discovery of vast reserves of blackband ironstone in 1802, technical progress and improvements in business organisation in the iron industry through the early 1800s (another set of factors which warn against an overly crude depiction of a 'two-stage' model), but principally the fuel savings made possible by J. B. Neilson's hot-blast process of 1828, along with relatively cheap labour, made west central Scotland the lowest cost pig-iron producing region in the UK [168:*150*]. Production (which had begun to rise from 1825), mushroomed from *c.*37,500 tons in 1830 to almost 700,000 tons in 1849, with Scotland's share of British output rising from five to 25 per cent. Gross capital formation in all branches of the coke-fired industry expanded from just over £1m. at the turn of the nineteenth century, to £6.5m. in 1840 [17:*74*].

The impact of this was profound, notably in the western Lowlands. There districts such as the Monklands, and from the 1840s the county of Ayrshire, and within them former rural weaving villages such as Coatbridge, were transformed as the iron companies sought to exploit their new-found cost advantage [288; 27:*93–116*]. Between 1828 and 1845 eleven new works were opened, nine of which were in Ayrshire, where no new ironworks had been erected since Glenbuck in 1796. The new transport infrastructure played a crucial role in Lanarkshire, notably the Monkland Canal (1793), its termini in Glasgow and Lanarkshire acting as 'nodes of industrial concentration'. So too did the Forth and Clyde canal (opened in 1790), which linked the two extremities of Scotland's industrial central belt, and eased the movement of goods both eastwards and westwards. Glasgow traders however, and from the 1820s manufacturers and shippers at Dundee, preferred to trade directly in bulk goods overseas using larger vessels which could not pass through the canal [173:*221*]. Canals however, of which there are only a handful in Scotland, were supplemented by the construction of a network of railways to succeed the earlier waggonways, which opened up new fields of ironstone and the splint coal which had replaced coke. The Garnkirk & Glasgow line, backed by coal and chemical interests in Glasgow and opened in 1831, was the first to directly challenge the canals, while the opening of the Glasgow, Paisley, Kilmarnock & Ayr line in 1840 enabled Lanarkshire iron companies such as the Bairds of Gartsherrie to move into Ayrshire [245:*44–96*]. Coal output, which had risen from 2 million to 3 million tons between 1800 and 1830, soared to *c.*7.4 million tons just after mid-century, with 76 per cent of this being mined in the west of Scotland [119:*26*; 258:*123*].

Iron was to provide the raw material of the Clydeside shipbuilding industry. Wooden ships had been built on the Clyde from 1711, but growth was slow thereafter, even during the 1780s and 1790s when the Scottish shipbuilding industry as a whole had failed to respond to the growing opportunities which rapidly rising trade presented, and Clyde-built tonnage accounted for less than 5 per cent of the British total as late as the early 1830s, although by this time Greenock and Port Glasgow firms had begun to build small wooden vessels powered by steam engines [170:*135*; 173:*234*]. Steam tonnage rose sharply between 1831–40 and 1841–50, and although the Clyde was putting out only 14 per cent of all UK shipping tonnage, its yards were responsible for 66 per cent of the tonnage of iron vessels in Britain [258:*125–34*]. Local engineering firms, associated with growing usage of and interest in steam engines at mines and mills, and that most of the country's fifty foundries and forges in 1813 were located in and around Glasgow (the earliest was Smithfield, 1732) and Greenock played a key part in this development, although it was after 1851 that west central Scotland became a major British engineering and ship-building centre.

Crafts' estimates of the proportion of male workers employed in 'revolutionised industry' in Britain in 1841 reveal the scale and intensity of the Scottish transition which had taken place. Three regions out of a total of eight in Scotland, Strathclyde (the largest – with Glasgow at its core – with a population of some 900,000, 34.5 per cent of the total), Central and Fife, and Tayside (which included Dundee), had markedly higher proportions of their populations in this category than the British average. The equivalent for England and Wales was six out of 43 [55:*4–5*]. At the same time, the Highland region had the highest proportion of males engaged in agriculture in Britain, and was on a par with English rural counties such as Bedfordshire, Herefordshire and Rutland in terms of the small numbers engaged in 'revolutionised' industries. Such categorisations however can create a picture of unwarrantedly stark contrasts: advance occurred on a broad front. What should not be overlooked is an expansion in the numbers of small-scale, often part-time and seasonal craft producers in the rural villages of regions such as Lowland Perthshire. In 1851 26 per cent of the occupied population of such villages were trades-people such as masons, carpenters, millwrights and tailors who played a crucial part in sustaining and changing the rural economy [320; 321]. In the larger towns building and allied trades came either second or third after textiles as employers of industrial workers [247].

Nevertheless, arguably by 1851 Scotland was more industrialised than the rest of Britain. Employment in manufacturing was slightly more significant north of the border than in the British economy as a whole. In 1851 43.2 per cent of the employed workforce in Scotland was in this sector, compared to a national figure of 40.9 per cent [184; 185; 178]. As has been indicated in the previous paragraph however, these numbers conceal major regional and intra-regional differences [165]. The service sector in Scotland was substantially smaller, although comparable in size to the industrial regions in the midlands and north of England [185]. The major exception was Lothian, which included the Scottish metropolis of Edinburgh: Lothian's economic structure, with its historic emphasis on the professions, commerce, personal services and consumer goods, and relatively small (but not insubstantial) commitment to manufacturing, was more like London and its environs.

An expanding economy, rapid industrial growth and a concomitant rise in national income however, which made it possible to sustain a population which had increased in size from some 1,265,000 in the 1750s to almost 2.9 million by 1851, produced less in the way of material rewards in Scotland than England. A smaller middle class and a lower level of service provision, especially marked in Glasgow and Dundee, is one indication of this; the consequences were losses of potential employment and countercyclical purchasing power [185:*15–17*; 247:*31–3*]. Another is that average Scottish wage levels were still below those of England by the mid-1800s, although the gap had been considerably reduced; indeed agricultural wages in Renfrewshire were as high as any in England, and those of carpenters in Glasgow and Edinburgh were close to those of some southern English towns [166:*942–3*].

On the other hand, Scotland contained the worst examples of rural poverty, in the Western Highlands and Islands, where poor crofters and cottars 'eked out a precarious existence close to the margin of subsistence' [76:*9*; 192:*22–35*]. Acting as a powerful corrective to the short-hand descriptions of Scotland – and Britain – as an industrial nation by the mid-1800s, was the great famine which followed the appearance of potato blight in 1846, and the consequent loss of population from malnutrition and disease, and above all, a massive surge in emigration. On the other hand, industrialisation in the central belt, and the opportunities for short-term employment this provided (crucially in 1846 and 1847, boom years in Scottish railway construction), was one of a number of reasons why the effects of crop failure were considerably less catastrophic in Scotland than Ireland.

3
Causes

Scotland's Industrial Revolution has been variously explained [146]. For some, the process was relatively uncomplicated. Scotland was part of the western world's international market system, entry to which had been obtained through geography and comparative advantage in textile manufacture. Overseas trade provided the key to nineteenth-century success in shipbuilding and heavy engineering which in turn owed much to the existence of rich deposits of coal and iron in the central belt. It is an argument which has been developed with various degrees of refinement and at a macro-economic level it makes much sense. Yet the emergence of Scotland as a major European industrial region was by no means inevitable and the reasons for it require fuller explanation, especially in the light of the differential pattern of regional development which has been identified within Scotland. It has been argued that the industrial regions in Britain each had their own internal dynamics and interconnecting characteristics which determined how they would respond to external challenges and opportunities [163]. Other British regions had declined after initial spurts, not only where hand-working had perished in the face of mechanised competition but even in east Shropshire where a successful iron industry and supporting transport infrastructure had been established [244]. A more telling comparison is Ireland which had had much in common with Scotland during the eighteenth century but by the 1820s had diverged to the extent that, with the notable exception of Belfast and the surrounding region, it was experiencing de-industrialisation [215; 230].

Although Scotland's industrialisation process was in many respects linked with that of England, it is not sufficient simply to apply currently favoured explanations for England's Industrial Revolution to her northern neighbour. Enough has been said already about the differences in the pace and nature of Scottish economic development. A more appropriate model for understanding and accounting for the early stages of Scottish industrialisation might be that developed by the late Alexander Gerschenkron who has argued in the context of European industrialisation that not only will backward countries industrialise fastest but that they will also be characterised by a number of other factors which are evident in the Scottish case. Amongst these are a greater emphasis on large plants and new technology, the importance of ideology and state institutions, an agricultural sector where productivity gains feed the population rather than acting as consumers of industrial products, and lower levels of consumption in the interests of a high rate of capital formation and the production of capital goods.

As has been indicated, external markets are central to most accounts of Scottish industrialisation in both its early and later phases. And there are strong grounds for arguing that overseas trade played a more active role in Scottish economic advance and industrialisation in the eighteenth century than currently favoured interpretations allow for England, although views on this are being revised [66; 8:*31–3*]. Indeed the creation of the British 'common market' in 1707 is the main reason why so many historians have in the past accorded the Union such a prominent role in their explanations for Scottish industrialisation [16:*13*; 144:*3*; 94].

After 1707 Scotland had had free access to England and was able to trade legally with the American colonies and Europe under the protection of the Navigation Acts, thus providing the conditions by which Scotland could resolve the balance of payments deficit which had brought the economy close to collapse in the immediate pre-Union years. Slowly at first – poor quality Scottish goods made little headway even in the protected markets – but much more rapidly from mid-century, export growth gathered pace, with a nine-fold increase taking place between 1785 and 1835, a rising share of which took the form of goods manufactured in Scotland. The focus of Scotland's overseas trade shifted from continental Europe towards the faster growing Atlantic economy, although the 'golden age' of tobacco was in large part dependent upon European prosperity and the tobacco habit, and in particular the preference in France, Glasgow's main customer, for Virginia leaf [68:*64–5*]. After 1800 Scotland's trade became increasingly divergent, with Asia, South America and Australasia taking their place as important trading partners by the 1840s [199:*149*; 173:*225–6*].

As far as the early eighteenth-century growth in Scotland is concerned much more telling is the evidence of the favourable impact of English demand for Scottish manufactures, for yarn and linen in the 1730s and 1740s for example [110:*35*]. The place of Ireland (which was also purchasing large quantities of yarn in the 1730s) in Scottish industrialisation tends to be overlooked. Yet in 1775 exports to Ireland were worth approximately double those going to America, while the volume of shipping was also twice as great [173:*215*]. By the later 1790s Ireland accounted for 20 per cent of the total value of Scottish overseas trade, which owing to its bulky nature utilised 30 per cent of the country's shipping capacity [49:*175*]. Scottish domestic exports to Ireland grew strongly from the 1770s and provided much-needed stability for Scotland's overseas trade and economic development during the years of the disruptive European and American Wars. There was a marked rise too in the export of the products of the more complex manufacturing industries of Scotland's Industrial Revolution, crown window glass, metal goods and chemicals, mainly vitriol. The impact of such sales however was generally dispersed. Coal was different. Of critical significance for the local economies based on the cluster of coal-mining communities on the north Ayrshire coast was the steep and sustained rise in demand for Scottish coal from Dublin and the north-east of Ireland from the 1770s, which between 1755 and 1795 accounted for between half and two-thirds of Scotland's coal exports [49; 294].

The significance of the transatlantic trade in tobacco, which reached its zenith in 1771, and the indirect benefits of this for industrial development in the Glasgow region, has already been noted. The 'vital stimulus' to the spectacular expansion of the linen industry between 1730 and 1775 and thereafter to 1800 by which time the quantity of stamped cloth had doubled to 24 million yards was external demand. This came mainly from England and the colonies, which between them took as much as 60 per cent of the total, although which of the two was more important cannot be accurately determined [110:*49*; 268:*618*]. Scottish-made linen found little favour in northern European countries which had established yarn and linen industries of their own, and where British commercial policy bred resistance to British manufactures [174:*14*]. East coast linen producers therefore depended upon the expertise and transatlantic links of London, Liverpool and Glasgow merchants to sell their cloth. However by 1829 some 30 per cent of Dundee's exports of what were mainly coarse cloths were being shipped directly, principally to the United States. It also went to satisfy the demand for slave clothing in the Caribbean which between 1765 and 1810 increased its share of direct exports of linen from Scotland from 23.5 per cent to 78.5 per cent [114:*10*].

The importance of the West Indies for Scottish trade and industry should be emphasised: sugar and rum imports (which continued to rise after the demise of tobacco, doubling between 1790 and 1815) supported major refineries and distilleries in Glasgow, Greenock and Port Glasgow while in 1775 exports to the region were worth twice as much as those destined for the mainland colonies. Its role became even more substantial thereafter, encouraging (along with Irish and North American demand) the establishment of numerous foundries and malleable ironworks. There were fifty in Scotland by 1813. At the end of the Napoleonic Wars the tonnage of vessels leaving Glasgow for the West Indies was 45 per cent of the whole, compared to 32 per cent and 23 per cent destined for Europe and America respectively [173:*227*]. Despite the emergence of continental markets for the finer quality products of the new cotton industry colonial links remained strong and indeed West Indian and to a lesser extent North American demand still dominated in 1810, with plain linens, haberdashery and fish being the main exports to the former [38:*202–3*]. Growing world markets aided by the freeing of trade and improved transport and financial arrangements in the first half of the nineteenth century facilitated the further expansion of exports not only of textiles such as coarse linen and jute but also for Scotland's minerals and metal products [191; 33:*17*]. Ships and shipping were other obvious beneficiaries – with Aberdeen-built schooners, clippers and barques being used in the South American and

Australian trades; by 1840 'the Clyde had entered the big-ship and big-company league' [173:*233*]. Often bigger businesses than some of the biggest iron, engineering and shipbuilding concerns at mid-century were a handful of Lowland whisky distillers for whom difficulties in the home market, including the anti-spirit campaign of the 1830s and 1840s, meant that sales overseas and to England were of the greatest importance [219].

It was from abroad that the Scots obtained a number of vital raw materials. The most important of these was cotton. Planter demands during the American War that Scottish vessels should also include some cotton in their cargoes led to what was virtually a halving in the price of raw cotton on the Clyde between 1776 and 1780 [88:*171*]. As was noted in chapter 2, this was one of the factors which appears to have persuaded numerous former linen and silk merchants and manufacturers to concentrate their activities on cotton spinning and weaving. Falling raw material costs as cultivation and the use of the cotton gin were extended in mainland America were no less crucial to the phenomenal growth of the industry in Scotland than Lancashire [42].

Linen, cotton's precursor, also depended on raw material imports, in the form of the traditional east coast trade in flax, which for reasons which are not entirely clear and despite repeated premium-backed exhortations on the part of the Board of Trustees was not widely grown in Scotland [111:*73–4*]. Hindsight suggests that the Trustees' failure in this regard may have been beneficial. In Ulster where most flax was home-grown this provided encouragement to proto-industrial families inhabiting fragmented agricultural holdings to continue small-scale peasant production and further sub-divide their land. In Scotland by contrast, a greater division of labour where spinners and weavers were removed from the immediate source of their raw material made it easier for merchant-manufacturers to centralise production [269:*266*; 115:*217*]. One reason for the lower levels of cultivation in Scotland was the elasticity of external supplies, although these were subject to periodic interruption. Dundee merchants were especially successful, increasing imports from 150 tons per annum in the mid-1740s to as many as 3,000 by the 1790s. They responded vigorously to wartime demand for sailcloth, hammocks and cheap shirtings by raising the port's share of British flax imports to 16 per cent by 1815. There was a further ten-fold rise in flax imports to Dundee between 1815–19 and 1845–49, although other east coast ports such as Arbroath, Kirkcaldy and Montrose also achieved rises which were faster than those of their English counterparts [174:*6–7*]. As pressure to reduce costs grew, culminating in 1832 with the removal of the long-established bounty on coarse linen exports, and as Dundee's manufacturers were driven towards the coarser end of the trade during the 1840s, attention increasingly turned to jute, a suitable but considerably cheaper alternative to flax and hemp [129].

One other category of import should be noted: Irish grain and to a lesser extent certain other agricultural produce including barrelled beef, pork and butter which were used primarily to provision Clyde ships at low cost [49:*126*]. Imported hides too were important for the Scottish leather industry, whose saddles, boots and shoes were made in Glasgow and Kilmarnock and exported to the colonies in considerable numbers. Ireland had been a marginal supplier of cheap grain to Scotland from at least the beginning of the eighteenth century, even though the Scots were net exporters. By the 1790s however imports from Ireland of oats and oatmeal alone may have been feeding some 40,000 people per annum, or 2.5 per cent of the Scottish population, although most Irish imports were consumed in the industrialising west [49:*97*]. Evidence that price rises were checked in Lanarkshire and Ayrshire during periods of relative scarcity suggests that in the main engine room of the emerging Scottish industrial economy the availability of Irish oats and oatmeal may have helped keep labour costs from rising and in towns like Glasgow contributed to the authorities' urgent efforts to keep the peace. When imports were checked, as they were in 1800 when the Irish ports were closed, the situation became critical [173:*231*; 305:*381*].

Although problematic, examination of the part played by the domestic market tends to confirm the emphasis placed on the stimulus of overseas trade. Between 1755 and 1801 the Scottish population increased at 0.6 per cent per annum, that is not much more than half the English rate and one third that of Ireland. More rapid growth occurred afterwards, in the decade 1811–21 for example, when it rose to 1.6 per annum. The annual average between 1801 and 1851 was 2.1 per cent [158:*12–13*]. Allied to the relatively slow rate of population growth in Scotland prior to 1800 and the widespread continuation of payments in kind for rural workers even where markets were in close proximity, detailed new evidence about Scottish wages, prices and consumption up to *c*.1780 suggests that the mass market for manufactured goods must have been slow to develop in Scotland [59:*256*; 131]. Exceptions were basic commodities such as salt, oil, candles and fuel, low-grade hand-knitted woollen cloth and hosiery, and home-produced linen cloth which successfully squeezed out Dutch and German linens. No firm data on the quantity sold in the domestic market is available however as the quantities of 'unstamped' cloth which were sold were not recorded, but a figure of around 40 per cent of total output would not be unreasonable [115:*211*]. The rise in household incomes which has been discerned after around 1760 but more noticeably from *c*.1780 did make for a clearly observable increase in the consumption of a limited range of commercially produced goods – primarily fashionable clothing (often English-made) as well as whisky and even watches and clocks. If as seems likely however such increases in expenditure were made possible by the new opportunities there were for women and children to earn wages in the proto-industrial textile sector (see chapter 4) rather than as the result of higher adult male wages then it must be concluded that the main spur was external rather than internal. The low-wage pattern of Scotland's industrialising economy con-tinued into the nineteenth century [33:*80–4*]. The laggardly nature of internal demand is confirmed by evidence from the iron industry where as has been seen domestic demand was insufficiently strong to sustain furnaces which had begun building during boom periods. Carron, with its reputation for quality ordnance as well as a vast range of domestic goods and industrial machinery, was somewhat exceptional [29]. Demand did strengthen as cast iron was substituted for wood and stone, but later and at a slower pace than in England, although significantly at least thirteen of the Glasgow foundry firms were also engineers [218:*12*]. In 1847 two-thirds of the pig-iron produced in Scotland was being exported [258:*121*].

Although caution needs to be exercised when assessing the role of the domestic market, it is also the case that domestic demand for manufactured goods was much more buoyant in Scotland than

Ireland [70:*19–20*]. Making a positive contribution was the uniquely rapid rate of Scottish urban growth and the concommitant demand this generated not only for foodstuffs, drink and clothing but also for building stone and slates, and coal for domestic heat and cooking. Lime burning too was a beneficiary, with urban needs adding to that of the agrarian sector [257]. Edinburgh, 'Auld Reekie', although still a major consumer of Scottish coal in 1800, was overtaken in the eighteenth century by Glasgow and the other towns in the Clyde basin as a generator of new mining activity in its hinterland, with output from Lanarkshire rising from 70,000 tons at most *c.*1700 to 550,000 in 1800 [108:*30*]. Wage levels tended to be higher in and around the central Lowland towns in the later eighteenth century, as a result of competition for relatively scarce labour between farmers and industrial and urban employers.

Demand was rising particularly strongly amongst the emergent urban middle classes whose numbers and wealth grew after around 1760, led, significantly, by overseas merchants. Although equally important numerically but less wealthy and of somewhat lower status was domestic commerce and distribution. A recent estimate suggests that as a proportion of the urban population the middle classes rose from 10–15 per cent in the 1750s to as much as 25 per cent by the 1830s [224]. Landed incomes grew substantially too and were translated into Adam house building as well as other conspicuous forms of consumption [37]. Both middle- and upper-class aspirations and material wants made clearly identifiable contributions to Scottish economic growth, the multiplier effects of their expenditure reverberating through urban services, agricultural output, notably of meat, and interconnecting roads. The building of Edinburgh's New Town commenced in the 1760s, followed by less ambitious schemes in other towns with a substantial middle-class presence [224:*112*]. The impact of specifically middle- and upper-class spending can be seen in the stupendous increase there was in paper production and books and coaches and even iron, for rainwater goods, railings and lamp-posts. Less obviously it played a key role in the emergence of framework knitting in the Borders and the rise in output from the 1780s of better-quality, higher-priced lambswool hosiery, establishing it at this early stage as an 'up-market' product [141:*26*; 199:*138*;

270:*61–2*]. Many products came from the south but over time Scottish manufacturers learned to compete, but less often head-on, preferring instead to find niche markets, as in the pottery trade where Scottish producers concentrated on making low-quality earthenware rather than china and tableware [292:*20*]. Complementary product development has been accorded a key role in explaining the success of the Scottish economy in the eighteenth century [30:*3*]. The concept is a good one, but too neat, as is the view that Scotland's post-Union success was a form of 'development by invitation' [290]. As will be seen, there was a strong competitive element too.

Those who argue that the Union was important for Scottish economic development and provided the environment in which industrialisation could emerge have a strong case. It can be made stronger by pointing to the other benefits which Scots obtained from the new constitutional arrangements which they put to good economic use [58:*166*; 56]. After 1707 Scots whose hopes of overseas success with the 1695 'Company of Scotland Trading to Africa and the Indies', which had foundered along with the dream of a Scottish trading colony at Darien in 1700, sought places within the East India Company. They found them too, in disproportionate numbers, and by trading on their own account many were able to amass and remit home small fortunes which were then invested in land and improvement schemes [232:*195*; 127:*112*]. The West Indies provided another and an increasingly important route after 1707 for ambitious young who sought means through the plantations or trade by which they could return with investment capital [58; 60:*238*]. Military service and army and navy provisioning also provided alternative lucrative sources of income for the younger sons of the peerage and gentry.

The British state played its part in other more conscious ways too. On the national (United Kingdom) scale attention has recently been drawn to the various ways in which the British government created an ordered trading environment. This was both at home (after 1746) and overseas as in the acquisition of various Caribbean and other islands and former French possessions in the 1790s [190; 60:*241*; 227]. State intervention was important for the linen industry which in spite of East India Company and Lancastrian opposition, was given favoured treatment in the English market largely owing to Westminster fears of political instability if economic hardship worsened [229]. In part growth derived from the efforts of the Board of Trustees to improve the quality of Scottish linen, while import duties provided an imperfect but nonetheless useful degree of protection for the fine linen industry in the west of Scotland. Crucial for the first decades of expansion of the coarse linen trade however in a fiercely competitive market in which the Scots were at a serious disadvantage against the Dutch, the German states and Ireland, were the export bounties payable from 1742 and 1745, the temporary removal of which in 1754 halved output in some districts [114]. Although not immediately and then only by default, Scotland benefited no less than England from the legislative framework which encouraged the fustian manufacture in Lancashire by reducing tariffs on non-Celtic yarns [229:*411*]. Although whaling was of only marginal significance for the Scottish economy, for some ports, notably Dundee, whale bounties generated employment and consequent local multiplier effects [169].

Although not linked directly with the Union, the role of English technology and its transfer to Scotland should be considered. Indeed in many respects it is the timing of the adoption of inventions such as the spinning jenny or Crompton's mule which accounts for the technological basis of the Scottish Industrial Revolution. Technically and organisationally Carron ironworks were modelled on Coalbrookdale. It was Crompton's mule which 'transformed' the supply position for the fine weavers of Glasgow and Paisley. Scotland's first cotton mill was built under the direction of a former employee of Richard Arkwright and an acquaintance of James Hargreaves, and indeed at least thirteen leading individuals involved in the formative period of the Scottish cotton industry between 1779 and 1795 owed much to their knowledge of, or experience in, English mill practice [18:*117*; 199:*186*]. Mechanised linen spinning followed the invention of flax-spinning machinery by Kendrew & Porthouse of Darlington in 1787. In coal, Newcomen engines were used at least until the end of the eighteenth century, James Watt's invention of the separate condenser in 1769 notwithstanding. English mining engineers were frequently consulted, while longwall working which spread quickly after 1760 was a cost-saving Shropshire technique. Tyneside provided the model for the numerous coal waggonways which were laid down in growing numbers from the 1760s, while English expertise proved vital during the construction of the first railways, with the Edinburgh & Glasgow line which was eventually authorised in 1838 owing virtually everything to the inspiration of the Liverpool & Manchester [245:*329–35*]. At the operative level, there is hardly an industry of any importance which did not owe something to the skills of workers who were imported from England, less often from Ireland and occasionally from mainland Europe.

Direct intervention and investment on the part of English entrepreneurs played their part too both before and during the initial stages of the Scottish Industrial Revolution. Lured by the promise of rich rewards from the exploitation of Highland resources a number of Englishmen had ventured north in the early eighteenth century, the most spectacular example being that of the York Buildings Company [63]. English involvement in the iron industry, whether defined by place of birth or source of capital, continued to be 'substantial' from 1759 until 1806 after which only the Coltness Iron Company originated south of the border [17:*75*]. Best-known is Richard Arkwright, doyen of the English cotton industry who was involved in the establishment of the large mills at Catrine, New Lanark, Stanley and Woodside. In common with other Englishmen who came north, in part Arkwright was attracted by Scotland's lower labour costs and the opportunity this would provide to undercut his Manchester rivals. Labour costs were low in the Borders too, where the framework knitting industry not only depended substantially on English customers and English technology – in the forms of the jenny, the mule and the hand-frame – but also on a 'significant' number of English entrepreneurs [141:*31*].

Thus far the emphasis has been on exogenous factors, although by no means exclusively so. Yet expanding markets were no guarantee of economic advance, even with state support. Indeed attention has been drawn to the risks which Union presented for the Scottish economy [74]. Economic success was not given, almost everything had to be fought for, hard [297:*175*]. It has been argued that this new context and the desire of Scots to emulate England's wealth provided an intellectual 'almost spiritual, influence very similar to that of religious ideas' [35:*221*]. While not wishing to ignore the pre-1707 and European roots of the Enlightenment in Scotland [3], it has been argued that by depriving many of the leadership class in Scotland of a traditional political role, Union did generate what has been called a process of 'inversion' whereby political energy was redirected into intellectual pursuits which focussed on national and personal wealth creation [34:*13*]. Enlightenment thought thus found a receptive and pro-active audience which ensured that one of its major concerns was the origins and causes (and effects) of the wealth of nations, while it has also been persuasively argued that the ideas on political economy which were developed by David Hume, Adam Smith and others were grounded in a lively debate about the relationship between rich and poor countries [149; 40].

In character the Scottish Enlightenment was intensely practical, with the Newtonian principles of order and simplicity as well as its other ideas and ideals (such as social progress) being widely diffused through the pulpit, lecture-room and parish and burgh schools [34; 316]. Rational enquiry and scientific method are considered to have had a positive effect on Scottish agriculture and industry. In this the Scottish universities, which had more students *c.*1800 than Trinity in Dublin and the two English universities combined, played their part [60:*237*]. In a broader but less specific way the practical outcomes of empirical observation can be seen in numerous instances of improvements made in the utilisation of water power by three generations of the Meikle family (*c.*1710–1811), or by Robert Thom, latterly manager of New Lanark who effectively introduced water power to Greenock in 1827. In Scottish textile mills many minor and usually unheralded modifications produced small but cumulatively significant incremental gains [164; 253:*482–6*]. All this serves to confirm the proposition that contrary to the views of an earlier generation of historians the impact of the Enlightenment was neither confined to a small elite nor to Edinburgh but was also felt in Glasgow for example, where James Watt's experiments with steam engines heralded the emergence in the region of skilled engineering, upon which the Clyde's reputation as an international centre of marine engineering and shipbuilding was largely built [255:*350*; 151].

Increasingly historians have been persuaded of the existence of other indigenous factors in Scotland which were favourable for economic growth and which provided some of the necessary conditions for industrialisation. The concept of prerequisites has some relevance in the Scottish case. While Scotland was on the periphery of northern Europe, in the period under review her geographical location worked advantageously. Proximity to the sea was crucial and during the 1600s and early 1700s traders were able to benefit from the fact that Scotland was closer to Scandinavia and the Baltic than anywhere on England's eastern seaboard, thereby easing the importation of timber, Swedish bar iron and flax for example. The last was imported into east coast ports such as Aberdeen, Arbroath and Dundee throughout the Industrial Revolution period and at a price which was considerably below that paid in inland Leeds [283:*11*]. England of course lay overland to the south. As opportunities in Ireland and across the Atlantic expanded from the later 1600s, the narrowness of Scotland's central waist (Glasgow and Edinburgh were only fifty miles apart) made the transfer of human talent, capital and goods relatively easy, even by road [263:*14*; 60:*227–8*]. Both Glasgow and Edinburgh drew on the same economically cohesive hinterland. The Atlantic crossing round the north of Ireland was easily accessible from the Clyde, and quicker by two or three weeks than for vessels which sailed from ports in the south of England. Freight costs were thereby reduced. Being out of reach of enemy privateers in time of war – at least until the Seven Years War – saved on insurance premiums [88:*145*]. The Irish Channel was narrow and relatively safe, while cross-channel shipping remained largely unscathed during the major European and American Wars [49:*17*]. The short crossing, made cheaper by the introduction of the steam boat in the early 1820s, and ensuing competition between rival companies made Scotland even more accessible for all but the poorest Irish emigrants, thereby swelling the Scottish labour market and reducing labour costs.

The weight that should be attached to natural endowments such as coal and ironstone deposits in the industrialisation process has long been debated by economic historians. Recent investigations have concluded that any explanation of the (British) Industrial Revolution in its European context which fails to acknowledge the part played by the elasticity of the supply of coal 'is likely to be incomplete' [238:*232*; 120]. In Scotland however the tendency has been to accord coal only a minor role in the eighteenth century and instead to underline the immensity of its contribution to the post-*c*.1830 heavy industrial phase of the Scottish Industrial Revolution. The great geological treasure-trove which lay beneath the surface of the counties of west central Scotland provided a cheap resource which was one of the keys to Scotland's world ascendancy in the production of semi-manufactured, standardised goods. Both coal and iron were essential inputs for the heavy engineering and shipbuilding industries, although these enjoyed their hey-day after 1850. The importance of Scotland's unique blackband iron ore deposits after *c*.1830 is unquestioned, although it should be noted that the invention of the hot-blast technique by J. B. Neilson in 1828 cut fuel costs rather than making possible the exploitation of blackband, which was happening anyway [168].

As far as coal is concerned however for the earlier period it has been argued (see above, chapter 2) that supply-side weaknesses in the coal industry caused it to grow more slowly than the rest of the economy, with fuel needs falling behind an erratic and periodically expensive supply [189:*134*; 30:*128*]. Traditional agents, human beings, animals, wind and water were the main sources of kinetic energy during the first decades of Scottish industrialisation. Broadly speaking this provides a striking illustration of Wrigley's characterisation of the Industrial Revolution in England as a transition from a 'traditional' economy in which specialisation occurred but the growth of which would ultimately be checked by its dependence upon finite and unreliable forms of organic energy. Critically, real incomes faltered and declined, but recovered once exponential growth occurred after being liberated by the exploitation of mineral fuel resources.

Recent work on the coal industry in Scotland however suggests that some qualification of the received view is necessary. Close examination of the alleged supply-side constraints has revealed that the evidence has been both misinterpreted and misunderstood. Coal taxes were not a burden but a boon for east coast coalmasters, underground water was no more a problem in Scotland than in other mining regions and was tackled with vigour, and the extent to which Scottish mines were starved of labour has been exaggerated [303]. Far from checking growth coal facilitated and encouraged it by, for example, satisfying the fuel needs of the burgeoning populations of the towns, the 'dynamic centres of economic change' in eighteenth-century Scotland, and thereby ensured that the movement of rural dwellers to the towns could be sustained. Peat *might* have provided an alternative, but this counter-factual possibility has yet to be explored. Neither the Dutch nor the Irish *experience* (as opposed to speculation about what might have happened) provide grounds for believing that it would have been a viable long-term substitute for the coal which Adam Smith thought was a crucial natural resource [319:*57–60*; Adam Smith, *Wealth of Nations*, Glasgow edn 1976, IV.viii.*42*].

Although coal was little-used in rural manufacturing, and the linen industry depended largely on hand labour and water power until the first steam mills were built in Dundee around 1790, the availability of an abundance of coal was a crucial factor in the emergence of Glasgow as a manufacturing centre in the eighteenth century and for the coarse linen-bleaching sector prior to the introduction of chlorine in 1788 [87:*7*; 303]. Scottish cotton firms were quick to exploit the advantages of steam which enabled them to locate more advantageously, in Glasgow, which was at the edge of the rich coalfields of Lanarkshire. Belfast's cotton industry, which was without this natural advantage, ceased to grow after the 1820s, partly for this reason [93]. Dundee's leading position within the textile area of east central Scotland was similarly associated with steam-powered spinning and the ease with which coal could be shipped in from the Forth and Newcastle, so that by 1839 Dundee's mills alone were using almost as much steam power as the rest of the water-powered Scottish linen industry [253:*523*]. The case for coal should be a balanced one however. The great age of water power in Scotland was *c.*1730–1830 and indeed the amount of power generated by water continued to grow at least until the mid-nineteenth century. A complex of factors account for regional superiority. Thus while some 69 per cent of the horsepower used in flax spinning in the 1830s came from steam, and inland mills (which had previously used water) tended to close, other factors such as size and degree of commitment and labour costs were other determinants of regional and local economic success [283].

The 'advanced organic economy' marched hand in hand with the emergent mineral fuel-based economy for many decades, as with Carron ironworks which used coke to smelt iron but water for the blast furnaces until the 1830s [253:*436*]. Nevertheless, in the leading sectors in the heartlands of Scotland's industrial economy and as the imperatives of regular working, continuous production and locational advantage grew in an expanding but production-cost conscious world market, the move was towards coal. Thus even though the woollen spinning mills in the Borders were largely driven by water wheels the fact is that large quantities of coal were required – and used – in the dyeing process, in spite of the expense of transporting it overland from Lothian pits [140:*46*].

The favourable if fortuitous resource base however had to be exploited. A great mass of evidence suggests that that function in Scotland in the eighteenth and early nineteenth centuries was carried out by a remarkably dynamic business class. The key players were drawn from the ranks of the landowners and the merchants, who in a country where there was a marked degree of social mobility were joined in growing numbers after 1707 by the lawyers, a profession whose social roots were to be found amongst the middling and upper gentry and lower nobility and who saw entry to the Faculty of Advocates as the best means of making a secure living and reaching the 'pinnacle of polite society in Edinburgh' [254:*36*; 60]. Arguably the critical internal factor both in the strengthening of the Scottish economy from the 1740s and the transformation which took place from the 1780s was the entrepreneurial response. Such a judgement however must be tempered by the fact that in Scotland as in England much more is known of the successes than the failures, and that of the last there were many more than is sometimes assumed [235; 101]. Nor is there anything remarkable about an argument which posits the importance of positive entrepreneurial action in economic growth. What is suggested here however is that in the Scottish case there were factors at work which gives this proposition a particular potency.

As was suggested earlier there was a powerful patriotic dimension to this modernising activity, at least in some quarters, the case of George Drummond, Lord Provost of Edinburgh for example [47]. Relatively low material standards and the desire to emulate English, Dutch and French lifestyles and to engage in conspicuous consumption, as well as a desire to take part in British politics acted as spurs, with a further impetus coming from the belief that as far as the lower orders were concerned employment – in manufacturing and fishing – and the virtues of hard work, thrift and sobriety would be an 'antidote to Jacobitism and disaffection' [57:*11*].

It was not only in Scotland that the connections between 'idleness' and wickedness were made by a ruling class intent on economic aggrandisement through a reformation of (lower-class) manners and, as will be seen in chapter 4, by revolutionising workplace organisation [194]. In staunchly Presbyterian Scotland however, where in 1790 only 2.5 per cent of the population were non-Presbyterian, it is possible that two features of Calvinism may have given additional encouragement to entrepreneurial initiative which, as close investigation into Scottish capitalist enterprise in the seventeenth century has shown, had an effective Weberian 'elective affinity' with Calvinist ethics [203]. The first was conscience, which resulted in constant self-criticism and a need to do better; the second was predestination, which demanded that the elect demonstrate evidence of their salvation. Together they 'implanted in the individual a high motivation towards achievement' [35:*226*]. It has been suggested that in Scotland this was expressed in ascetic economic action rather than the creative arts [33:*28*].

Scottish landowners, of whom there were roughly 7,500 in the early 1800s, have been described as 'the most absolute in Britain' [264:*218*]. After 1707 they used their enormous political and social authority to build upon their late seventeenth-century efforts to reform Scottish agriculture and improve the quality of Scottish manufactures, although no longer through parliamentary and privy council acts. Instead they sponsored and drew on the financial assistance provided by quasi-state bodies such as the Board of Trustees, the Royal Bank of Scotland and the British Linen Company (founded in 1746), 'the only chartered bank in the United Kingdom that had as its purpose industrial development' to which it contributed by extending the putting-out system by extending credit and issuing its own notes [270:*69*; 45:*92–9*].

When assessed in quantitative terms, the impact of most of the landowner-led schemes referred to above is rather slight and largely of short-term significance. In the longer run however the establishment of institutions such as the Royal Bank and the

British Linen Company was important, with both contributing to Scotland's total banking assets, which rose from less than one-third of a million pounds in 1744 to over £12m in 1802; over the same period bank assets per head rose from £0.27 to £7.46. They contributed therefore to a banking system which many historians believe played an important and integral part in the emergence of the Scottish industrial economy, but which can be hard to quantify. Nevertheless comparison with the English banks of key indicators such as banking density and per capita assets – and stability – reveals a Scottish banking system which was better able to mobilise capital and considerably more responsive to the needs of industrialisation [25:*106*]. The banks' contribution was less in the provision of long-term capital, although their role here should not be underestimated, especially for the iron industry and agriculture and in the provision of social overhead capital, mainly in the form of turnpike roads and canals [45:*232–3*].

More important was the Scottish system of cash credits, first introduced by the Royal Bank, and the small note issue (as well as bill-discounting, which was the main form of lending by the private provincial banks). Such services were critical in an economy which was specie-hungry but which was served by a banking system which ensured that the localities were provided for, often through local, usually merchant- and trader-led, initiatives. These were behind the formation of the provincial banking companies (forty-five of which were set up between 1747 and 1836) or the provision of branches by the public banks [220; 301:*34–41*]. Older reservations about the contribution of Scottish banking to economic development (as opposed to banking practice) cannot be ignored however [31:*xxi*]. Current indications are that personal finance, often obtained from within kinship networks, and the ploughing back of profits were the major sources of long-term capital in the Scottish Industrial Revolution.

In spite of their enthusiasm and even the 'particular Calvinist fervour' with which they went about their business, as has been noted, faced with inadequate demand and considerable tenant resistance the agricultural Improvers made little headway in the first half of the eighteenth century. On the other hand it is worth emphasising the point (alluded to in chapter 2) that investigation into the counties of Lanarkshire, Ayrshire, Fife and Angus has revealed that two important changes were occurring beneath the surface of rural society which were to be of crucial importance when market demand picked up. First, there was a widespread erosion of rentals in kind towards cash rentals, a development which had the effect of driving tenants towards direct contact with the market. Secondly, the move towards single tenancies accelerated, a process which would later make much less troublesome the process of large-scale estate reorganisation.

When market circumstances did become more favourable from *c.*1760 and after a lull again from the early 1790s the response of the commercially aware agricultural sector was in one sense astounding (although given their commitment to reform, this should not really occasion surprise), the yield of oats in Scotland increasing between 200 and 300 per cent between 1750 and 1800 for example, compared to an English figure of 50 per cent [82:*57*]. Meat output may have multiplied by a factor of six between the 1750s and the 1820s. Such productivity and output gains have to be accounted for, as without them the industrialisation and urbanisation of Scotland simply could not have taken place on the scale and at the speed which they did. The strains on Scotland's balance of payments imposed by the need to import grain and expand credit for manufacturing would have been too intense [31:*xx*; 33:*14*]. Allowance of course has to be made for inter-county and even estate-by-estate variations in both crop yields and husbandry methods, but generally speaking rural Lowland Scotland was swept by an unprecedented wave of improvement from the 1760s and 1770s (and again in the 1790s), funded by large sums of capital which were to be recouped by steep rent rises demanded of tenants who were now wholly exposed to the vagaries of the market as the last vestiges of 'in kind' rentals were all but eliminated [82:*44*].

Change was manifested in the transformation of the landscape, arguably more thoroughly than anywhere else in Europe in the eighteenth century (although the process was not completed until the 1830s and 1840s), with enclosure sweeping the countryside and the older scattered rigs or ridges of land being replaced by regular fields divided by hedges, ditches or dykes. Single farm steadings became the norm. Crop increases were obtained by spreading lime and dung on a greater scale than ever before, while there was a marked acceleration in the use of sown grasses and, although more laggardly, of turnip husbandry too. Regional specialisation became more marked. Whereas in 1750 the Scots were drawing on England and northern Europe for examples of the most advanced husbandry by 1830 Scottish agriculture was providing models for others to copy – the Lothian 'factories for making corn and meat' with their highly efficient labour forces for example, while versions of the improved Scots plough were the most common sort of ploughing implement found in Sweden [266:*303*; 273:*88–9*].

Considerable debate has surrounded the question of the respective contributions to agrarian reform of the tenant farmers and landowners. The fact is that in their various ways the contributions of both were essential. Yet there are good grounds for arguing that at the heart of Scotland's rural transformation from mid-century was the existence of a landed class which was determined to break with past practice and 'impose a new [and rationally based] economic and social order' [82:*61*]. Their authority which in several cases encompassed extensive territories which stretched into several counties but more often involved smaller estates was derived from several sources. These were political power; feudal rights and privileges which were only abolished in 1747; rights over land use, which operated through a system of fixed-term written leases (mainly of between five and increasingly, nineteen years) and included powers of summary eviction. Unlike many other parts of Europe there was an absence in Scotland of peasant land rights which could slow the process of rural transformation. Unlike Ireland therefore in Lowland Scotland multiple tenancies were more easily reduced and movement off the land – a factor which encouraged social mobility and was a necessary pre-condition for urban growth – was thereby encouraged [248:*84*; 60:*234*]. Finally there was the law of entail, which buttressed landed security and authority.

If landowners initiated change and were largely responsible for financing it a class of able factors, agents and land surveyors such as Peter May planned and managed it [2]. Tenants, drawn from the stock which had been thinned in the first half of the century, instituted the reforms, acting in accordance with, but adapting in the light of local conditions and experience, the detailed 'improving' leases which were central to the programme of agrarian reform [273]. Implementation was enforced by a strategy which combined coercion with incentives which typically included new farmhouses and assistance with improving costs. In the case of the more substantial farmers however, mainly in the Lothians and south-east but also in Angus, Fife, Ayrshire and elsewhere, the literate and educated tenants of the newly built two-storey farmhouses whose social status rose along with farm size and produce prices, coercion was hardly necessary. Although not immediately or without disputes with landlords about over-ambitious rent levels particularly after the two crises of 1772–73 and 1783–84, there is considerable evidence to suggest that they were themselves becoming ardent advocates of improvement by the 1790s and early 1800s [82]. It was lower down the social scale that hostility to consolidation and innovation and the impact of commercialisation was encountered. The extent and significance of such opposition is the subject of ongoing debate. Easing the process of change however and going some way to explaining the extraordinary success of the Scottish agrarian revolution was the fact that unlike Ireland, the landed class was largely 'an indigenous and hereditary elite'. Through the 'delicate ties of hierarchy and dependence' which operated in the fields of parish education, poor relief and church appointments (of ministers) landowners were able thereby to soften and blunt the edge of opposition and ensure what was by and large a peaceful transition to fully fledged capitalist agriculture [266:*303–10*; 71].

It is evident that in their pursuit of wealth and status Scottish landowners did not confine themselves to agricultural reform, although outside of the sphere of rural enterprise their enthusiasm tended to wane after *c.*1790 [264:*230*]. Scottish landlords committed themselves on a broad front to maximise the income from their estates [248:*88*]. Coal mining was the most notable example, although fixed capital investment in the industry accounted for less than 2 per cent of gross national (British) investment in the 1810s and 1820s. Scotland was one of those regions in which a large number of coalowners continued to take a direct interest in mining, although this was truer of Clackmannan, Fife, the Lothians and Stirlingshire than Lanarkshire and Renfrewshire [120; 108:*141–59*]. In extent but not in scale limestone was not far behind. Transport improvement was another arena in which land-owners excelled. Harbour development provided an outlet for estate produce and minerals, as in the cases of the major Ayrshire coal ports of Saltcoats, Ardrossan and Troon as well as several on the Forth which were opened or extended to tap the burgeoning demand of the east coast for domestic and industrial coals shipped coastwise. More significant however was their support for road improvement via the 350 or so turnpike trusts which were established between 1750 and 1840, but most of which were concentrated within the critical growth period *c.*1770–1800. In textiles their role was useful but not decisive, except perhaps for cotton where landed initiative was often important in attracting and siting (but rarely running) the early country mills [18:*117*; 186:*212*; 118:*75–6*].

Unqualified, the category 'landowner' is something of a misnomer in the sense that in Lowland Scotland the land market was remarkably fluid – much more so than in Ireland – with the large number of small estates making it relatively easy for merchants and others who had acquired non-landed fortunes to penetrate the landed sector [70:*21–2*]. Unlike Ulster, the propertied elite in Scotland was infused with fresh capital, skill and experience, which were directed towards the establishment of cotton mills for example. Landowners with mercantile interests were more likely to be directly involved in such ventures, while the social and economically ambitious Glasgow tobacco merchants, most of whom owned an estate at some stage of their life, were credited by Adam Smith with being 'the best of all improvers' [248:*88–9*; 18:*117–18*; 68:*27–33*; Smith, *Wealth of Nations*, Glasgow edn 1976, III.iv.*3*; i.*423*]. While this remark may somewhat exaggerate the contrast between the new men and the longer-established landowners (although Smith also distinguished between small proprietors, who he favoured, and large proprietors, of whom he was critical), there can be little doubt that some of the most spectacular developments in coal mining in the Glasgow region in the later eighteenth and early nineteenth centuries were the result of merchant endeavour. This was not only in terms of scale but also in the determination of those concerned to rationalise production (see chapter 4).

It was not simply or even mainly as landowners however that Scottish merchants played what was a crucial role in the Scottish industrialisation process. Nowhere perhaps can the results of their energy and determination to succeed be better seen than in Glasgow, whose merchants engaged in colonial *entrepot* trade 'as the fastest way of creating mercantile wealth on a meagre economic base' [172:77]. From a low pre-1707 level they increased their share of UK imports of tobacco from just under 5 per cent between 1708 and 1711 to 16.6 per cent by 1725, much to the discomfiture of Bristol and Whitehaven. The locational advantages noted above were exploited by a series of merchant partnerships who were prepared to engage in widespread customs fraud, spurred it seems by a passionate anti-Union sentiment, and thereby undercut their English rivals [241]. Later expansion was based first upon their ability to draw on the credit of the new banks (see chapter 2) but much more importantly by ploughing back profits and mobilising, through high-yielding bonded loans, the funds of the middling classes in and around Glasgow. It rested secondly on their exploitation of the advantages of the store system and the direct purchase of tobacco, quickly-negotiated volume sales at relatively low prices which were paid for in cash by resident French buyers.

Further honing Glasgow's 'intimidating' competitive edge was the rapid turnaround time of the port's shipping fleet which over time increased in both size and efficiency [88]. By 1800 it comprised 500 vessels, which included 60 per cent of Scotland's ships in the 200 tons-plus category, necessary if it was to maintain its command of the transatlantic and eastern trades [173:229]. In Glasgow therefore a commercial framework was established which had two main consequences for that phase of industrialisation which took place prior to the era of heavy industry. The first was the backward integration of mercantile capital manufacturing. The second was the continuing role of merchants as overseas traders, importing raw cotton for the cotton industry for example, and providing market opportunities for other west of Scotland producers [38:191–4].

Impressive though Glasgow's entrepreneurial record is, what should be emphasised is that similar characteristics appear to have been commonplace across the Scottish business community. Local and regional studies, of which many more are required, confirm this as well as pointing to the heterogeneity of the entrepreneurial pool. The Borders woollen industry for example was led and funded not by merchant capital but by small fullers and dyers whose capital was drawn largely from slow accumulations of personal savings; Aberdeen's granite manufacturers tended to have been journeymen and labourers; in Edinburgh it was artisan producers who had been at the forefront of the new individualistic economic order in the earlier 1700s [140; 107; 60]. Dynamic, observant and with acutely sensitive business antennae Scots entrepreneurs were willing to learn from and imitate best practice elsewhere. It was they who imported most of the technical know-how and skills referred to earlier from England, the Low Countries, France and Ireland. There were some spectacular instances, such as the rapid adoption of wool-preparation machinery and spinning jennies in the Borders, and the mule (driven by water after 1790 following William Kelly's adaptation of it for this purpose) which gave the Scottish cotton industry a short-lived technological lead. There were also almost certainly many more mundane cases which have not been recorded, the 'many late inventions for abridging labour' which one contemporary noted in Glasgow in the 1790s [305:366]. Indicative of Scottish concern to keep abreast with developments elsewhere were the flax spinners and linen manufacturers of the east of Scotland who regularly toured the English linen districts to study the operation of mills and factories there and where appropriate to adopt or adapt new technology to local conditions [191:14; 128]. The function of 'captains of Industry' according to Peter Carmichael, a leading Dundee mill and factory manager, was not to invent, which was a 'mockery and a snare', but to 'produce the best article at the cheapest rate'. Even so, from within the synergetic environment of agrarian and industrial transformation significant Scottish modifications and inventions were forthcoming, as has been seen. The contrast with Ireland where pressures for labour-saving innovations were less intense, is striking. Scotland, a country of imitators of the 1750s had within a few decades become a society which in the world context was able to produce major innovators.

Identifiable too is a commercial aggressiveness which is to some extent belied by the concept of complementary economic development. Some Scottish businessmen did compete directly with England in Britain and in third markets. Tobacco is one example.

Whaling is another [169]. From the outset strenuous efforts were made by Carron Ironworks to compete in the English market, while Ayrshire and Lanarkshire coalmasters competed with Cumberland in the Irish coal trade throughout the eighteenth century and beyond. Even in the linen industry, where there was a significant element of regional specialisation in Britain and Ireland in the eighteenth century, in the early nineteenth century many textile firms in the Dundee district were engaged in an intense struggle with English producers in Barnsley and Leeds.

Although Scotland offered certain advantages such as lower wage rates, and when conditions were favourable businessmen could exploit unique natural resources such as blackband ironstone in Lanarkshire and granite in Aberdeen, a more prudent course was often to scrutinise the marketplace for openings where competition was less fierce. The responsiveness of Scottish entrepreneurs to new opportunities was noted in chapter 1. Such a manoeuvre was not always possible, as the cotton masters discovered in the 1820s and as a result they had to resort to increasing production at lower costs first in the coarser lines and then in the crowded finer end of the market [30:*109–10*]. Product differentiation did take place however, in linen for example, with premium prices being paid even for coarse linen in London before and during the Napoleonic Wars which was of high quality or distinguishable from the mainstream products by width, finish or colour. This continued to be a feature of the marketing strategy of the more successful firms [301]. One of the most remarkable examples is provided by the woollen industry which in the 1820s was struggling in the face of Yorkshire competition. The inroads made by the Scots in the UK industry owed much to the efforts of enterprising Borders manufacturers who vigorously attacked the growing market for fashionable twill (or tweed) cloths by concentrating their attention on high quality wool and superior design, especially in the use of bright colours [240]. In Aberdeen, Crombies, makers of high-quality overcoatings, were to become the best-known woollen cloth producer in the UK [177:*80–2*].

The conceptualisation of the Scottish Victorian economy as one built upon two interlocking foundations therefore has much to commend it. On the one hand were the 'generalists', the producers of coal, iron and cotton; on the other, later but overlapping, were the 'specialists', who depended more on skill and specialisation – in some textiles, woollens for example – but more importantly ships and heavy engineering [33]. By 1850 they were jointly yoked and the great Scottish Victorian economic miracle had dawned. Both of course depended on expanding markets world-wide and Scotland's geological resource base. Human beings were the agents who created the organisational, financial and technological links between the two. They also provided the labour, the main focus of the next chapter.

4

Social aspects of the Scottish Industrial Revolution

That social change lay at the heart of the Industrial Revolution has been argued by a long line of historians. It can encompass a remarkably wide range of human experience. The main focus of this chapter will be the ascendancy of market relations both within and beyond the workplace. This, it will be argued, provides a particularly apposite means of understanding the nature of the Industrial Revolution in Scotland. The chapter however will also examine linked issues such as the standard of living and the role of women and children, although it should be noted that in these and other relevant areas of social change in Scotland in this period – crime and popular culture for example – only minimal research has been carried out. Owing to limitations of space the complex question of class will be skirted around.

As was noted earlier, in early modern Scotland where rural links were stronger and more widespread and most households had at least a scrap of ground for personal use, 'life-time labour was relatively less important' than in England [157:25]. The situation described towards the end of chapter 2, with Scotland having achieved by the later 1840s the status of an industrial nation, makes it clear that during the previous century or so profound social changes must have been taking place, in both the distribution of the population and the nature of the workforce.

Reference has already been made to the rate of urban growth in Scotland in the eighteenth century. By 1800 Scotland had risen to fifth place in the European urban league and was second only to England and Wales by 1850. Whereas England's urban growth in the eighteenth century was rapid but continuous and protracted,

Scotland's was 'abrupt and swift' [75]. Nowhere was this more so than in Glasgow, which by 1821 had overtaken Edinburgh and become the second most populous city in Britain outside London. Between 1801 and 1851 Glasgow grew more rapidly than any of the other major towns. The other early pacemakers in urban Scotland after *c.*1750 were also commercial and manufacturing towns such as Paisley, Kilmarnock and Falkirk, the slowest growing of which more than tripled its population between *c.*1750 and 1821 [75:*35*]. Between 1801 and 1831, the percentage of the Scottish population in towns of 5,000+ rose from 21 per cent to 31.7 per cent, a rate of advance which was faster than at any time in the nineteenth century. But as late as 1861 less than 40 per cent of Scots lived in towns with more than 5,000 people.

   This however ignores the smaller towns and in particular the 'planned villages', deliberately created settlements which were usually integral parts of plans to improve and restructure individual estates by removing unwanted tenants and cottars and promote economic growth by acting as markets and local centres of employ-ment and moral improvement [267]. Created by landowners and bodies such as the British Fisheries Society (f.1786), planned villages had precursors in the pre-Union era, but the most concen-trated period of activity was between *c.*1770 and 1819 when some 283 were established, mainly for spinning and weaving and the provision of rural tradesmen, but also as fishing stations [196; 221]. Widely distributed, the importance of their place in early Scottish industrialisation requires to be emphasised, even though some – notably the west coast fishing villages such as Lochbay in Skye – failed to flourish. Attention has more recently been drawn to other forms of small-scale urban development in rural society, and the extent to which new (non-'planned') settlements appeared, or existing small villages whose populations were in the 100s expanded [82:*40, 152–3*]. In the 1830s some two-thirds of the country's handloom weavers worked in such smaller towns, vil-lages and settlements [222:*22–5*], although they were by no means confined to textiles. In Caithness and elsewhere in the north-east, fishing villages such as Ferryden near Montrose grew at a rate 'roughly on a par with that of the industrial cities' in the first half of the nineteenth century [137; 54]. Thus examination of the size of the urban population alone can wrongly lead to the conclusion that

'Scotland was not yet [by 1841] an industrial country' [192:7]. The existence of significant population densities outside the towns serves to confound such an impression: only 28 per cent of the population lived in parishes classified as agricultural alone, whereas 52 per cent were in urban-industrial parishes, that is in districts such as North Lanarkshire where coal-mining or iron-working was carried on (and where densities were highest), or in some textile areas which were also fertile enough to sustain a sizeable farming population, as in the linen-producing counties of Angus and Perthshire.

Urban growth and urbanisation however were only one part of a wider and dramatic process of population redistribution whereby the Highlands and North (and after 1811, the Borders) lost ground to the central Lowlands. In the mid-eighteenth century, Perthshire, which contained both a Lowland as well as a Highland division, was the most populous county; the central belt accounted for only 37 per cent of the country's population. Five of the top six most populous counties were in the east [199:*87–97*]. By 1821 the central belt's share had risen to 47 per cent, almost wholly at the expense of the north, migrants from whence flocked south [158:*22*]. Short-distance migration was more important however. The main source of Lowland growth was Lowlanders, with a town such as Paisley obtaining most of its 15–18,000 immigrants over the period *c.*1760 to 1800 from the adjacent rural counties of Ayrshire and Renfrewshire [162:*293*]. Although there is some uncertainty about it, the movement of substantial numbers of Highlanders into southern Lowland towns and cities can probably be dated to the later eighteenth century, although as early as 1700 some 6 per cent of Greenock's population comprised Highlanders [119:*475*; 315]. Lanarkshire had become the biggest county by 1801. The western Lowlands as a whole continued to amass its share of Scotland's population, housing just under one in three Scots by 1851. The share accounted for by the eastern Lowlands fell slowly between 1801 and 1851, although it was only after mid-century that it dropped below that of the West [119:*306*].

An integral part of the process of industrialisation in Scotland was temporary migration, a swelling flow of labour from the southern and eastern Highlands to the Lowland plain which had its roots in Highland poverty and the temporary demands for (mainly female) hands on the part of farmers in the eastern Lowlands in particular. For males there were the Clyde fisheries, but military employment, albeit by its nature irregular, was of much greater importance, notably so during the French Revolutionary Wars. By the early 1800s however opportunities for temporary work, the earnings from which provided critically important supplements to household budgets, were being created by an expansion of domestic service in the towns (which had been a major attraction from early modern times) as well as in industrial complexes such as bleachfields and on a range of labouring tasks such as railway construction which drew migrants from a widening field which included the Outer Hebrides [84]. Similar but not identical pushes and pulls also encouraged immigration from parts of Ireland. This began on a seasonal basis but from the 1790s the flow of permanent migrants strengthened, as first hand weaving and from the 1820s the Irish domestic spinning trade in south Ulster began to decline, the last in the face of competition from machine-spun yarn [51]. The troubled aftermath of the Irish rising of 1798 also caused many to flee to the west of Scotland. With periodic potato crop failures from 1845 the numbers rose sharply so that by 1851 there were over 207,000 Irish-born living in Scotland, a 90 per cent increase since 1841.

Their impact could be profound, in social and cultural as well as economic terms. There are suggestions that Ulster-born spinners and weavers may have given Scottish radicalism a new potency in the later 1790s and *c.*1816–20 [289]. By mid-century half of Dundee's linen industry's labour force was Irish-born (in part drawn by the mills which had contributed to the demise of hand-spinning in Ulster), as were half of the coal and ironstone miners of Coatbridge [51; 27:*178–9*]. The Irish thus added further to the pool of surplus labour in the Scottish industrial centres after *c.*1815, although a recent investigation study of assimilation patterns of Highlanders and the Irish into Glasgow in the mid-1800s suggests more Irish migrants found their way into skilled occupations in the heavy industries than has been assumed hitherto. On the other hand they had much less success than the Highlanders [260]. Prepared to accept lower wages, the Irish tended to be drawn into easier-to-enter trades such as handloom weaving, where they accounted for around 30 per cent of the workforce by the later 1830s. They were utilised by employers who exploited the opportunities their presence provided to introduce 'blackleg' labour into coal mines for example, or do the more burdensome jobs such as ironstone mining, along with certain unskilled work where they were more numerous than the Scots. Resentment on the part of those sections of the indigenous population who felt the direct effects of low-wage competition and the fact that the religion of the majority of migrants was Roman Catholicism heightened social tensions in mining and weaving towns and villages in Presbyterian counties such as Lanarkshire and Ayrshire; these were intensified where Irish Protestants (at least 25 per cent of the immigrant stream) brought with them a militant Orangeism [27; 207]. On the other hand, if population pressures and economic change and even collapse (see below) in some areas were creating misery in parts of the Highlands, the rural Lowlands and the burgeoning towns after *c*.1815, that discomfort was in turn partly relieved by a rising tide of emigrants from Scotland.

However, while the rate of outflow was faster than from contemporary England it was considerably less than Ireland's and lower than it was to be from the end of the 1840s. Prior to that, ideological opposition which took concrete form in the shape of the 1803 Passenger Act had prevented emigration from the Highlands on the scale that had periodically marked the later eighteenth century. In addition the poorest retained their traditional attachment to their small plots of marginal land until utter destitution – and landowner concern that they would be burdened with the cost of maintaining the surplus poor – forced them to relinquish their grip [167; 84]. In the Lowlands a few thousand handloom weavers found assisted passages but most emigrants were former rural rather than urban dwellers, and appear to have been drawn largely from the ranks of tenant farmers and independent country town and village mechanics and craftsmen, although agricultural labourers were by no means absent. For the materially dispossessed however the only realistic option was to move to the rural villages and urban districts. Despite atrocious conditions (see below) they were not without their attractions [139]. One of them was waged work at rates of pay which were higher than in the countryside, another, 'excitement and carnal joys' [19:*144*].

The introduction in a short space of time of a cluster of new technologies, and accompanying organisational changes, including the factory and new forms of worker control, are central to some definitions of the Industrial Revolution. The rational management of labour it has been argued required 'the fiercest wrench from the past' [237]. Such conceptualisations are essential for an understanding of the nature of the Industrial Revolution in Scotland, where the transmission of the work ethic and the control and effective management of labour were particularly acute problems, as 'owing to the country's "late start", they had to be tackled on a wider front' [304:25].

Such a view is not held universally however. Some historians have assumed that not only was there an adequate supply of labour in eighteenth-century Scotland but also that Scottish workers were sufficiently docile and suited to the requirements of industrial society [210:96]. Fuelling this suggestion is the belief that the working out of Calvinist theology at parish level instilled appropriate attitudes and values into the consciousness of the plebeian poor. Hence the reformed church in Scotland unwittingly became the 'handmaiden' of nascent capitalism, by 'accustoming the workforce [in early modern Scotland] to social discipline, and by stressing the value of order, restraint and hard work' [231:19]. It has been suggested that the process was further eased by the organisational superiority of the putting-out system in the linen industry. Here the increasing separation of farming and waged work in rural manufacturing created a 'quasi-proletariat which found little difficulty in adapting to the age of greater specialisation and more rapid growth in textiles after *c.*1780' [74:36].

Nevertheless there is a growing body of evidence which demands substantial modification of such views. It should be emphasised however that the controversy relates to the first decades of industrialisation. As will become apparent later in this chapter, the labour supply position was transformed from the second decade of the nineteenth century, thereby securing one of the main foundations of Scottish industrial success in the following decades, low labour costs.

Seventeenth- and early eighteenth-century developments in manufacturing and forays into centralised production notwithstanding, in the mid-1700s the employing classes in Scotland were confronted by acute shortages of skilled labour (as was seen in chapter

3) and the problem of recruiting and shaping a disciplined army of wage workers. Indeed the difficulties of transmitting skills in and supervising the quality of handloom weaving has been advanced as one reason for the failure of proto-industry in Scotland to develop in those parts of the Highlands where pastoral agriculture predominated, elsewhere in Europe classic proto-industrial territory [311]. Wage rates in Scotland were lower but inefficient production methods meant that labour costs could be higher. Earlier attempts to overcome such difficulties had met with little success. Indeed it has been speculated that notwithstanding the compensations of urban life, the means by which rural dwellers in Scotland had been prised from the land by Scottish landlords may have bred an attitude of hostility to further change, resulting in the creation of a 'deeply hostile and conservative labour force'. Such a trauma was not experienced in Scandinavia, nor in Ireland where domestic manufacturing and agriculture went hand in hand [273:92].

The published evidence certainly supports this and suggests strongly that although the kirk's teaching had penetrated downwards as far as the level of the artisan and the small tenant-farmer, throughout the ranks of the labouring poor, where male illiteracy levels could be twice as high, it had generally fallen on deaf ears. The illiteracy rate amongst female labourers and servants in the eighteenth century – around 90 per cent – was even higher [157]. Although the putting-out system lay behind the great expansion of the output of the linen industry in the eighteenth century, the proto-industrial model is of limited value only in accounting for the emergence of urban mill- and factory-based manufacturing in Scotland [311].

A telling but representative example of the enormity of the challenge in what quite simply was a momentous exercise in social engineering facing Scottish capital comes from Carron ironworks. Labour (journeymen as well as foremen) for virtually all the building work had to be brought north from England [29]. Workers recruited locally for the '*English* foundry' (the emphasis draws attention to a powerful antipathy towards southern incomers) were tainted with the habits and attitudes of what was described as a 'Country of Idleness' and necessitated a battery of measures designed to break the 'cake of custom' in both Scottish coalmining and ironmaking but also where other industries such as flax and cotton spinning were concerned [296:*228*; 109:*37*]. Widespread though they were, irregular attendance and a tendency to mix work with play, drunkenness, 'theft' of perquisites and workers' informal collective agreements about output and pay of course were not uniquely Scottish problems, although recent research has begun to unearth their extent north of the border, with urban journeymen's collective organisations dating back to the 1720s for example, and coal miners' even earlier [123].

As was suggested above, the Scottish dimension appears to have been the urgency and force with which such constraints had to be and were tackled by ambitious entrepreneurs as market opportunities beckoned. The widening of horizons in Glasgow in mid-century for example produced a series of confrontations with the restrictive practices of the trade incorporations as employers with an eye on colonial markets demanded the right to employ non-freemen and as many workers – male or female – as they required [305:*363–4*]. State action, through the Board of Trustees' successful attempt in 1751 to break the legal hold of linen and hemp weaver guilds over apprenticeships and labour mobility, achieved little in the short-term, but demonstrated a clear recognition of the importance of a flexible labour market [111:*79*]. Legislation was also enacted in the interests of capital in 1775 and 1799, and not, as is commonly asserted, to 'emancipate' Scotland's life-bound coal workers, but rather to free their masters' hands over wages and workrates without the interference of powerful combinations. Significantly, amongst those at the forefront of the employer-led campaign of 1773 and 1774 to change the law and which drew specifically on Enlightenment writers and the advantages of a low-cost economy were coalmasters who were involved either in the export of coal or who like the Glasgow merchant-landowner Archibald Smellie of Easterhill were selling in competitive markets and whose principal objective was to cut labour costs [302:*68–9*].

Centralised workplaces appeared throughout the Lowlands of Scotland with increasing frequency from the 1740s and 1750s as employers sought to regularise output. Most of these were relatively small concerns. Lowland paper mills typically employed ten workers for instance, roughly the same as limeworks. Insurance valuation data suggests that there were 'numerous' small firms in cotton spinning in the 1790s. Yet there were also significant numbers of unprecedentedly large works. Principally but not exclusively however these were cotton mills, bleachfields and ironworks which from the outset often employed many hundreds of people – sometimes over 1,000 – in one place.

For the larger more regimented workplaces Highland and Irish migration played a critical role in compensating for the initial reluctance there was throughout Lowland Scotland to enter cotton and spinning flax mills, although Highlanders could sometimes prove to be unwilling industrial workers [52]. The requirement for piecers and the need to cut production costs and if possible drive them below those of their English competitors provides a compelling explanation for the widespread use of the labour of pauper children, 'often the conscripted shock troops of a generally reluctant Scottish industrial army'. Not only in textiles but in printfields and the acutely competitive trade of hand nailmaking they were frequently employed under restrictive conditions which were on a par with the worst found elsewhere amongst the industrialising countries of the world [296:*244–6*].

Recent attempts to recover the 'British' Industrial Revolution have emphasised the importance of women's and children's work, a factor which has usually been missing from economic accounts of the period which measure only the male contribution to labour productivity [6; 7; 8]. Although the subject requires much more detailed investigation, even in the current sketchy state of knowledge there can be little doubt that their role in Scotland's early economic transformation was even more substantial, if not crucial.

It is important that the context is properly understood as it may provide part of the explanation for early Scottish industrialisation which has been overlooked hitherto. As in England, there was a low sex-ratio throughout the early industrial period. There were four other significant factors however which appear to have made for an even more favourable supply-side situation in the female labour market in Scotland. The absence of a discernible fall in the age of first marriage (*c.*26–27 during the later 1700s) which was slightly later than is suggested by the wider English range of 23–27, and a celibacy rate which may have been double that south of the border are two. A third is the number of single poor females in Scotland but more important the impact of the Poor Laws which 'kept potential workers alive' but at a level which normally meant that they had to find some sort of paid work in order to survive at anything above subsistence levels. The critical factor however appears to have been the fact that in numerous plebeian households throughout Scotland male earnings were insufficient to maintain a family during long periods of the life-cycle [131:*349–56*]. The part-time earnings of female (and child) members of the household were therefore critical and in the case of textile employment could fairly readily be fitted into the Lowland farming cycle. In short Scotland's relative backwardness and the low living standards which prevailed for the greatest part of the eighteenth century created one of the necessary conditions for the Scottish economy's great leap forward in the later eighteenth and early nineteenth centuries. Largely because of the conjunction of a relatively low rate of population growth and a rapidly growing economy in the three decades after 1760 it seems highly unlikely that the reserves of underemployed male labour which have been reported for England were to be found. There are some tantalising suggestions that between the second and towards the end of the third quarter of the eighteenth century there was a substantial increase in the number of days worked by male rural labourers in Scotland. Three hundred days apparently was 'not unusual' [131:*281–2*]. Similarly, changing work patterns rather than the introduction of new technology go a long way towards accounting for the increased output of rural artisans in the later 1700s and first decades of the nineteenth century [321].

What was urgently required was not only a docile labour force which would quickly adapt to the new patterns of workplace organisation, including in some instances new technologies, but also one which was cheap. Low wages was not the sole reason for employing females in Scotland. Other key variables were the condition and nature of markets, the prevailing state of technology and simply employer preference, to name but three, but it does seem that cost considerations overrode everything else [304]. There may have been one other slight but unmeasurable advantage in employing Scottish women in such numbers. Ironically in the light of Scotland's relative poverty and periodic visitations of dearth, particularly in the Highlands, evidence is coming to light which hints at the possibility that Scottish women workers may have been stronger than their English counterparts, a phenomenon which was observed at the time by Andrew Ure. The typical working-class diet in the eighteenth and early nineteenth centuries was restricted and involved the consumption of copious quantities of oatmeal, but it also produced the tallest males in the UK up to 1850, and it seems, fit women [131:*243*; 181:*3*; 304:*30*].

Given the economic circumstances described above, part-time employment in the ubiquitous hand-spinning trade was probably welcomed (initially at least) with open arms. There is no better instance of the symbiotic relationship between rural impoverishment and the needs of overseas merchants than in the 30,000 worsted stocking knitters there were estimated to be in Aberdeenshire in the 1790s. The expansion of flax spinning (and therefore of the linen industry) in the eighteenth century had been almost entirely dependent upon female hand-spinners while at most bleachfields a majority of the workers was usually female [111]. A similar situation prevailed in the burgeoning trade of muslin sewing in the west of Scotland in the later 1700s. Yet it is in the 'revolutionised' sectors where the utilisation of female labour attracts most attention. Following the mechanisation of flax spinning the male to female ratio was 100:280: in no other part of the UK was the proportion of female labour so high, despite the fact that hand spinners in the heartland of the flax trade, Forfarshire, had initially resisted mill work. In Dundee during the 1840s, female employment had increased by a factor of 2.5 and male employment by 1.6; by 1851 no other large Scottish town had a majority of its females in industrial employment, with increasing numbers being employed as powerloom weavers, each female's two looms by the 1830s turning out as much cloth as three or four male handloom workers [247:*29*; 284:*21*]. In cotton too, there was a noticeable difference, with child labour levels being higher in Glasgow than Lancashire. Women and girls constituted 61 per cent of the workforce in Scottish mills, compared to 50 per cent in Lancashire [9]. Andrew Ure calculated a ratio of 100:209. In the two decades following the passing of the Factory Act in 1833 however there was a significant drop in the proportion of child workers in the Scottish cotton industry (to 2 per cent by 1847), to below Lancashire levels, partly as mill proprietors sought to divest themselves of the costs and effort involved in providing education facilities. Juvenile and female labour provided an ample and cheap substitute [19:*142*].

Although, as might be expected, the bulk of female and child employment was in textiles, there were other areas in which they had a relatively large presence, as in coal mining for example, with some collieries employing twice as many females (mainly as bearers) as males in the eighteenth century, although this was a continuation of pre-industrial practice [159]. Even in 1830 however some 12 per cent of underground workers in Scotland's mines were female (contrasted with a British figure of 4 per cent), with most of these being concentrated in the east, in the Lothians and Fife [120:*334–5*]. Far and away the most important of the non-textile sectors was agriculture, where the proportion of females employed was significantly higher than in England and Wales [72:*98–9*]. Again their economic role in this vital sector should be acknowledged. Formal female participation in the industrial labour force almost certainly peaked during the 1830s however, even allowing for various forms of under-recording on the part of census enumerators; the rising heavy industries and coal and ironstone mining which were to dominate the Victorian Scottish economy had little need for women workers. Outside the cotton industry where their numbers rose after the 1837 spinners' strike and accounted for a quarter of female employment in the counties of Lanarkshire and Renfrewshire in 1851, and the coarse textile town of Dundee and some other smaller centres, women most commonly found themselves steered towards domestic service and casual work [133:*15–54*; 181:*23–4*].

The well-known concepts of combined and uneven development can legitimately be applied to Scotland [250]. The concentration of whisky distilling in larger highly capitalised plant and stills following the clamp-down in 1823 on the small peasant-run illicit Highland stills serving local markets was accompanied in some districts by an increase in casual work in peat-cutting and carrying – although contraction between 1835 and 1844 had the opposite effect [219:*89*]. A more striking instance of the unevenness of the industrialisation process in Scotland is provided by the Shetland hand-knitted lace industry, which, organised on out-working lines, was first established in the 1830s at a time when in Lowland

Scotland the numbers in handloom weaving were reaching their peak (c.84,000) prior to their rapid fall following the much more widespread use of the powerloom after 1840 [5:*57–60*; 222:*48*]. Such a generalisation however conceals both regional and local variations within the Lowland area. Thus whereas by 1838 most weaving of heavy and plain cotton was done on powerlooms located in and around Glasgow, handloom weaving remained the mainstay of the linen industry 'well into the second half of the 19th century' [284:*21*]. While in the 1830s the number of powerlooms *per capita* was greater in Scotland as a whole than England, in the east, where four out of ten handloom weavers in Scotland were located, the amount of cloth produced on the powerloom was small relative to the rest of the UK [223:*220*]. The continuity of the handloom however was rarely to be equated with the survival of the independent existence which weavers had valued during the so-called 'golden age' of the 1770s and 1780s, although handloom weavers in Dundee continued to resist the introduction of steam power into the 1830s. Employer fears that the introduction of powerlooms might result in a bout of Manchester-like machine breaking was one factor which delayed their use [128:*80*]. Few customer weavers survived the proletarianisation of the industry and then only in the rural districts, and weavers engaged on fabrics where there was a premium on skill, as in the case of the damask weavers of Dunfermline, were more often than not proprietors of their own looms. Indicative of the direction in which the bulk of the trade was going was the Borders woollen industry where largely for technical reasons powerlooms were not widely used until after 1850. By the end of the 1820s however most Galashiels handloom weavers were employed in loomsheds or factories, as they were in Aberdeen and Montrose in the following decade. In Arbroath and Forfar on the other hand the proportions were much lower, largely owing in the last case to the fact that most weavers were also small landholders [284; 301]. In Galashiels on the other hand wages held up reasonably well whereas handloom weaving generally had in the words of the Inverurie weaver-poet William Thom, become 'a mere permission to breathe'.

What has necessarily been a narrowly focussed discussion, concentrating on textiles, supports Maxine Berg's contention that there was no 'through road' to the factory system. This is con-

firmed when the investigation is widened to include other industries such as iron where the imposing high-walled closely super-
vised works at Carron or the Camlachie Foundry in Glasgow can
be contrasted with the many small non-specialist foundries with
their handfuls of versatile workers [15:*204*]. Even Carron was
employing outworkers in nailmaking, in two or three scattered
communities [29:*78–82*].

Yet certain common tendencies can be identified, which lead
towards the conclusion that in the core regions industrial capitalism in Scotland was exerting similar pressures on large sections
of the working class. Paternalism for example is said to have
pervaded industrial relations in Scotland in the eighteenth century,
its most common and public manifestation being the setting by JP
courts of wage rates after representatives of both workers and
employers had been heard [122:*281*]. Its break-down however has
been traced to 1812 and identified with a conscious shift of
opinion about the role of combinations (which continued to be
legal in Scotland after 1799) amongst west of Scotland employers
in particular, and increasingly influential younger Whiggish
lawyers who were adherents of Adam Smith and the free market.
There were of course notable exceptions, as in the Midlothian
coalfield where landowner paternalism persisted well into the
Victorian era, colliers there remaining 'subdued and uninvolved'
during the west coast miners' agitations of 1844 and 1849–50
[147]. Although the catalyst – the struggle over handloom weavers'
wages – concerned English workers too, it is notable that the
confrontation took place in Scotland.

'De-skilling', and efforts to loosen worker control over certain
key processes, occurred on a broad front during the 1820s and
1830s as employers in coal mining, cotton spinning and weaving,
calico printing and flax heckling, to name but four trades, sought
in the face of fierce worker opposition, to improve their competitive
position [305:*376–8*]. In this the Scottish employers were simply
part of a nationwide 'contest for the control of work between
capital and labour' [4]. In Scotland however the indications are
that there may have been a harder edge to the industrial struggles
of the period. The 'abominable assumption of power' on the part
of the Associated Colliers of Scotland was one of the factors used
to justify the Government's proposals to amend the repealed

Combination Act in 1825. Few groups of employers in industrial Britain were to exercise as much control over their workers through their proprietorship of vast areas of the Scottish coalfields and the works, housing, schools and associated buildings they erected upon them as Scotland's coal and ironmasters such as the Bairds of Gartsherrie. For them an aggressive paternalism in industrial relations was designed to induce 'militaristic obedience' from their employees [27; 28; 179:*143*]. Perhaps the most telling example however is the Glasgow cotton industry where vitriol was thrown and vitriolic songs were sung during an extended period of often violent conflict during the 1820s and 1830s over workplace control which culminated in the cotton spinners' strike of 1837 [19; 121]. Unforgiving in their victory and strongly anti-union in their sentiments, the cotton masters turned their backs on collective negotiation, preferring instead to fix wage rates arbitrarily. While the outcome in the short-run was to keep wages low, in the longer term their uncompromising strategy led to non-co-operation on the part of their spinners and weavers, with the result that by the 1880s production costs had risen above those in Lancashire [10].

A similar revolution occurred in the countryside. In the Lowlands in the second half of the eighteenth century the older complex and hierarchical rural structure, within which were intertwined communal obligations and restraints over individual action, was replaced by a simpler one in which single tenants had greater power, and their now land-less and wage-dependent subordinates less. Over the period *c.*1750 until the 1840s but at a variable pace in which regional and local differences were marked, a rural proletariat stratified by task, status and income was created. Among the more obvious social divisions, sub-tenants were gradually removed from the rural landscape, and cottars (who had formed as much as one-third of the rural population in the 1690s) swept away in the last decades of the eighteenth century and the early years of the nineteenth. As sheep and to a lesser extent cattle farming advanced in south Lanarkshire, upland Ayrshire and highland Angus, displacement occurred on a scale which is reminiscent of the better-known Highland clearances [82:*140*]. As in the towns, combinations of agricultural workers found themselves under attack, with hours of work and working conditions rather than wages being the main sources of employer-employee disputes [155]. The new regime was most striking in the large factory-like farms of the Lothians and parts of Fife, less so in Ayrshire and Galloway and those parts of Lanarkshire and Renfrewshire where dairying prevailed, organised on the basis of family farms; uniquely in the Lowlands, in the north-east, there was an extension of crofting [138].

Change however was tempered by continuities, in forms such as the long-hire of servants and payments in kind which went some way towards shielding the newly fashioned rural proletariat from the vicissitudes of the market, although not from a legal system which worked to the advantage of the farmer [71; 155:*32–3*]. Recent research has shown that smallholdings and farms of up to 100 acres were much more common outside the south east in the nineteenth century than received wisdom would allow. This was for a variety of sound economic and social reasons, such as the need to slow the pace of removal in order to encourage tenants to experiment with new methods and to avoid outbreaks of rural resistance [85]. The adverse effects of radical change upon those whose footholds on the land disappeared were masked not only by the survival of such smaller farms but also by the shelter and opportunities for work. This could be in manufacturing or, in certain localities, in agriculture itself, on a daily, waged basis made possible by the existence of the landowner-generated rural villages referred to earlier. The pain therefore of rural transformation was probably felt less acutely, at least before *c.*1815. Post-Napoleonic War depression and a shift in the demographic variable (see below) heralded a period of rural change which it has been argued was 'characterised by discontents and agonies inflicted on the lesser people and on much of the old tenantry' [139:*15*]. Even so, the re-envigorated march of Scottish industrialisation from the early 1830s was mopping up the worst rural unemployment. The modern consensus is that conditions in the Scottish countryside were less uncomfortable than in certain areas of England which in 1830 experienced the 'Swing' riots.

Although there were clearly a number of ameliorating factors at work in the Lowlands, in the Highlands the effects of agrarian change were considerably more disruptive. The influences which generated landowner-led change were similar (as too were some of the effects, such as the elimination of multiple tenancies), at least until the last decades of the eighteenth century. By then a process had begun whereby Highland landlords tended to abandon their former 'proactive' role in favour of a reactive response which saw a switch of focus from aggressive commercial development of their estates to one of commercial pastoralism and recreational capitalism [202]. In the decades following the 1760s commercialisation and voracious demand for Highland produce from the towns and manufactures of the Lowlands and England transformed Gaelic society in which kinship ties and traditional as opposed to legalistic concepts of land-holding had been paramount [201:*70–1*]. Agrarian 'improvement' proceeded through the dismantling of the traditional township, group settlements 'which had formed the basic communities of Gaeldom since time immemorial' and their conversion into large commercial sheep farms which would typically employ only half a dozen shepherds as demand for and the prices of wool and mutton soared [84:*33*]. The inhabitants of the former townships were cleared and relocated on small sub-subsistence plots – the crofting communities which were especially numerous in the north and west, including the Inner and Outer Hebrides, but less so in south Argyll and Highland Perthshire where farms of 40–60 acres were more common [76:*1–4*]. Removal created social tensions which periodically erupted into violence as those threatened with dispossession fought to defend customary land rights and to resist being removed to the coastal villages. There they were expected to adopt the requisite 'industrious' way of life urged upon them by landowners and their agents whose moral purpose gave added legitimacy – and ruthlessness – to their reforming policies [242; 273].

Until the second decade of the nineteenth century the new system was sustained by the widespread adoption of the potato as a food crop and the by-employment generated by demand for products such as fish, whisky and kelp. Indeed extractive industry and manufacturing, both full- and part-time, was seen as an integral component of the region's transformation: low wages would give it an edge in external markets while the employment created would assist in retaining the displaced population who would cultivate and add value to the marginal land upon which they had been resettled. Although contemporary hopes that

Sutherland could be converted into a Lancashire of the far north came to little, frequent attempts were made during the eighteenth century to implant manufacturing industry in the Highlands, sometimes with a modest degree of what was usually short-lived success [242]. Whatever the ultimate fate of kelp, the profits from it which were not channelled south to absentee lairds enriched and enlivened the lives of resident proprietors. At the same time the modest earnings from it introduced many cottars to the money economy, raised living standards and, crucially, acted as a cushion against harvest failure which occurred in roughly one year in three. Road and canal construction too contributed to the early viability of the region, with the opening of the Crinan Canal in 1801 for example ensuring that the massive slate quarries in Lorne maintained their dominant place as the principal provider for Lowland builders. Although the rate of population growth in the crofting region declined after 1801 and was much more modest than in Ireland or even the rest of Scotland (which had been exceeded in the Western Isles and adjacent mainland areas in the previous half-century), numbers continued to rise until 1831.

The march of industrialism therefore was not uni-directional. Nevertheless regional specialisation and the concentration of water- and steam-powered spinning mills and weaving factories in the core producing districts led to a slow retreat from the outlying regions. Cotton mills in the countryside outside the main centres found themselves squeezed out, as in Galloway and Aberdeen in the later 1830s and 1840s respectively [199:*186–7*]. Between 1811 and 1851 something in the region of 33,000 jobs in textiles (full- and part-time) were lost in Aberdeenshire, with textile employment falling over the same period from 30 per cent of the county's population to 3.6 per cent, while in parts of Fife too there were unquantified reports of unemployment amongst hand-spinners in the later 1820s as mill spinning spread [287:*80*]. The consequences of the withdrawal of secondary production, which was occurring elsewhere in the marginal regions of Britain as industrial capitalism matured, had their most devastating impact in the Highlands. The collapse of the kelp trade and the fall in cattle prices after 1815 encouraged a further wave of land reorganisation and commercial sheep farming in islands such as Lewis, Rhum and Muck as landlords exploited one of the region's remaining comparative advantages [136; 76:*18–19*]. Despite seasonal and permanent migration from the islands and the Western Highlands there remained countless numbers 'of congested crofting settlements with no apparent potential for economic development', yet whose occupants had through their introduction to imported 'luxuries' been drawn into a market economy in which they could no longer participate. The worst conditions were found on those estates where kelping had been of most importance, and had tended to induce the steepest rises in population – an exceptional 118 per cent in South Uist between 1755 and 1811 for example [244:*220*; 167:*38*]. In Orkney and Shetland too it was in those parishes in which little kelp was gathered and burnt that destitution occurred [280:*101–4*]. While historians debate the extent to which the ultimate fate of the Highlands and Islands was inevitable, there can be little justification for challenging the conclusion that in no part of the British Isles did market forces and industrialisation wreak so much havoc or leave such human suffering in their wake. The relationship between the Industrial Revolution and living standards has long been debated by historians. Although the subject has inspired rather less close investigation in Scotland than it has in England and Wales and suffers from the absence of a Scottish cost of living index, what work has been done suggests that the pattern in Scotland was somewhat different [282]. Whereas in England after around 1750 conditions worsened (though not – significantly – in the industrialising counties), in Scotland during the first decades of the Industrial Revolution living standards appear to have risen, slowly at first but then strongly, although this has to be set alongside the wretched conditions which prevailed beforehand. In the European context this was unusual. Some groups of workers did remarkably well. Lowland agricultural workers living in the proximity of towns, which had favourable effects on wage rates, improved their standard of living by between 40 and 50 per cent. Indeed most centres of manufacturing either in urban or rural locations saw improvements [131:*339–40*]. More intense economic growth from *c*.1760 and the relatively low rate of population increase appear to have been the main determinants of rising *per capita* prosperity in the central Lowlands and parts of the Highlands. In the north west and Hebrides however where manufacturing had made few inroads, rapid population growth, rising rents and recurrent subsistence crises 'placed a firm brake upon the scope for material advance' and in this sense had more in common with the south of England, large parts of Ireland, the Low Countries and Scandinavia [282:*199*; 131:*341*]. There are doubts too about how far the north-eastern plain beyond Aberdeen had benefited, as well as those parts of Dumfries and Galloway which were outside the textile parishes [131:*339*]. Almost everywhere however, even in the industrialising Lowlands, it would appear that living standard improvements owed less to rising real wage rates and increasing employment opportunities for adult males than to the massive expansion in paid work for women and children which was referred to earlier [131:*353*]. Exceptions were bachelors in urban areas who could find accommodation free or at low-cost, as well as skilled workers. In both cases however prosperity was dependent upon the ability of those concerned to find employment for at least two-thirds of the year. If so they did a lot better than unskilled married men with children to support.

From the early 1790s the Scottish picture mirrors more closely that for south of the border although the evidence currently available for Scotland provides no support for the more optimistic positions in the standard of living debate. Broadly speaking the period of the French and Napoleonic Wars appears to have been one of stagnation. The pattern however was complex: until the early 1800s the real wage trajectory for many groups of workers maintained its upwards course, and in the case of agricultural workers continued to do so until 1814. Industrial workers achieved marginal gains at best, while others – notably the unskilled – experienced losses. Dilution in the weaving trade, first amongst the weavers of plain fabrics, began a long-term fall from 1808. Cyclical upturns as in 1814–15 provided only temporary relief from a protracted and steep fall in money wages and a proportionate rise in deductions which affected all weavers and their families who were drawn in increasing numbers into a trade which demanded longer hours to make a living irrespective of the fabric worked [222]. As wartime prices rose, in weaving as in other trades where the bastions of skill were increasingly hard to defend or non-existent anyway the critical variable was the demographic one. The rate of population increased, doubling on average in the first fifty years of the nineteenth century (and rising even more rapidly between 1811 and 1821). Surging demand and price inflation encouraged a further wave of enclosure and consolidation in the countryside in the 1790s. There was accordingly an addition in the numbers of former cottars seeking accommodation and waged employment either in the rural villages or cities such as Glasgow.

Peace brought price deflation and after around 1820 wage increases for skilled workers which produced real income rises over the period 1814 and 1830 of between 25 per cent (for coal miners) and 43 per cent (Glasgow machine makers) [282:*204*]. The last (obtained by other groups of skilled urban journeymen as well) represented a considerable improvement over the early 1790s; by and large agricultural workers too managed to improve on their *c*.1790 position, mainly through price falls. Such gains however were not shared by the unskilled who in Glasgow were poorer in 1830 than they had been at the start of the 1790s (but better off than in the 1760s). Indeed a survey of average real wages for workers in nineteen occupational groups suggested that they continued to drop until 1839 and contemporary accounts from elsewhere in Lowland Scotland report very basic diets in which as in the previous century oatmeal and milk were prominent and meat scarce. Symptomatic of irregular employment and growing hardship within the household was the opening in 1813 of Glasgow's first licensed pawnbroking shop, 'a phenomenon of the Industrial Revolution' [22:*181*]. However, with a price index having been generated only for Glasgow (1810–*c*.1840), it remains to be proven whether this pattern was repeated throughout the urban centres [135]. Demobilisation however was discharging additional bodies into Scotland's already growing reserve army of labour which, after a Court of Session ruling in 1819 inspired by Malthusian concepts of political economy, could no longer depend upon the old Poor Law for relief, although this was proving to be entirely inadequate in the urban areas anyway [212]. It seems reasonable to suppose therefore that its divisions were to be found in all the main industrial towns and cities.

The immediate impact of the Industrial Revolution on Scotland's urban sector is curiously under-researched: better-known is the period after *c*.1850. Recent work however has begun to expose a remarkable level of urban disamenity. This is particularly visible in Glasgow, the second city in the empire which had seen a massive rise in middle-rank affluence in the later eighteenth century and the first two decades of the nineteenth which manifested itself in prestigious housebuilding schemes to the west of the city centre [225]. Yet at just this point in time Glasgow's environment was becoming the most lethal in Britain, the overcrowded, unsanitary and unenvied host to epidemics of cholera and typhus [22]. 'Fever' mortality during the typhus epidemic of 1837 was twice that of Liverpool and not much less than three times Manchester's rate [89]. The city had the country's worst mortality rates which rose steadily from 1821 and by 1835–39 were twice the 1801 level. Not age-specific, the crude death rate figures which peaked at 39.9 per thousand between 1845 and 1849, are indicative of an overall worsening of conditions in a city in which textile employment predominated [22:59]. Edinburgh (which also had a sizeable commitment to artisanal and some large-scale manufacturing as well as its share of squalor) was some way behind, with a rate of 25.4 per thousand in 1841 although its mortality rate for fever was worse than the worst English towns. Perth, Leith and Dundee vied for third place, although by 1861 Dundee had almost drawn level with Glasgow [119:*377–83*]. Qualitative contemporary comments suggest that by the early 1840s Dundee, with the smallest middle-class component of the main Scottish cities and which by 1851 had a marginally higher proportion of Irish-born immigrants but a much lower percentage of Highlanders, was becoming yoked with Glasgow as a (much smaller) site of similar human degradation [281; 300]. A 'one-industry' low-wage town, it was even more vulnerable to cyclical downturns than Glasgow, but not Paisley which in the depressed economic conditions of 1841–42 suffered perhaps the greatest distress ever experienced in a large British town [271:*25*]. In their ability to counter these cyclical troughs with middle-class spending power neither was comparable to Edinburgh or Aberdeen with their much more favourable economic structures. In 1851 for example 35.08 per cent of Aberdeen's industrial employment was in textiles and clothing, whereas in Dundee the comparable figure was 61.36 per cent [247:*36–7*]. Squalor and the other attendant ills of rapid urban growth were not confined to the large manufacturing cities. On a lesser scale the mushrooming coal and iron 'frontier' towns of Lanarkshire and Ayrshire, which prior to the 1830s had often housed pockets of struggling handloom weavers, suffered proportionately from the problems of inadequate water supplies, overcrowding, disease and levels of drunkenness and petty but savage male-led crime which in Airdrie in 1848 may have surpassed those of Glasgow [27:*117–44*]. Crime and its prosecution in Scotland are topics which in historiographical terms are in their infancy, although current indications are that the Scottish pattern was not unlike that of England. Judging by the measure of High Court precognitions (pre-trial proceedings carried out by the Procurators Fiscal), there was a marked increase in crime over the period 1812 to 1850 which tended to fluctuate with the economic climate, peaking in the mid-1820s, the later 1830s and mid-1840s. Suggestive of economic hardship on the part of the most common groups of offenders – labourers, carters, weavers, colliers and other urban workers in low-wage or irregular employment – is the rising proportion of crimes which were acquisitive in nature, 75 per cent by 1830 [103]. Petty theft was commonplace, particularly amongst females.

If the incidence of 'public' crimes, which include combinations and strikes and disturbances during lock-outs, riot and other forms of disorderly conduct, can be interpreted as a crude measure of economic fortunes and social relations, then there is little doubt that large parts of Scotland were experiencing acute difficulties in the second, third and fourth decades of the nineteenth century. While during the eighteenth century the Scots were not the 'uninflammable' kirk-cowed people they have been described as by some historians, most (but not all) popular protest was relatively easily contained by the authorities. In character it was conservative and backward-looking and legitimised by the notion of the 'moral economy', although one writer has argued that in Edinburgh the 'integrative' riot had been superseded much earlier by riots in which class hostility was evident [160:*330–1*]. Industrial disputes had become more bitter by the end of the century, as in the case of the Glasgow weavers' dispute in 1787 which had resulted in eight weavers being killed by the military, but even so the consensus is that Scottish Radicalism in the 1790s was short-lived and a pale shadow of its Irish counterpart. A powerful set of reasons have been advanced to explain this 'failure', if indeed this is what it was [78].

By the 1810s however a number of these factors no longer applied. As has been seen, material standards for many were worsening and paternalism in industrial and social relations was being replaced by a hard-headed belief in the primacy of political economy. The results can be briefly outlined. The handloom weavers' leaders' faith in the courts up to 1812–13 meant that Luddism had remained an English phenomenon – until 1817 when threats of a visit from 'General Ludd' were made to stocking makers who undercut agreed rates during a brief wave of machine breaking in Jedburgh [103:*16*; 123:*94*]. More telling was the so-called 'Radical War' of 1820 which was linked with English unrest and followed the Peterloo massacre. Even so, it has been argued although not proved conclusively that 'events in Scotland were more extensive and serious than anything in England' and indeed what needs to be emphasised is the scale and extent of disturbances which occurred from 1819 onwards into the early 1820s and beyond, many of which can be linked either directly or indirectly with the changes associated with the extension of market relations and industrialisation [122:*286*; 302]. Handloom weavers were to the fore, but cotton spinners, coal miners, tailors and others were also involved in a series of riots which swept parts of Glasgow and the West of Scotland. With neighbourhood and community often providing the platform for action participants were concerned with a variety of grievances ranging from rights of way and dog taxes to workplace control to wage rates [305:*387*]. The geographical spread of protest however was wide, with serious risings in opposition to clearance in both Ross and Caithness in 1820 [242:*212–5*].

Not all disturbances were specifically targeted however. From the later seventeenth century the monarch's birthday had in Lowland Scotland been a major carnivalesque occasion in the restricted calendar of popular culture. More noticeably the locus of class-based social tension in the later eighteenth century changed as the distinctly class-conscious middle and upper classes withdrew from an occasion which had previously been communal in intent. There were years in the first half of the nineteenth century – in 1819 and 1821 in Glasgow and in Greenock in 1847 for example – when it produced some of the ugliest riotous behaviour ever experienced in urban Scotland. Here as elsewhere the last hours of the day often became an 'apparently senseless orgy of fire and fury' (and fatalities) as crowds in which youths and the unskilled were prominent directed their hatred towards sometimes terrified urban elites in an unprecedented torrent of cathartic release [302]. The demands for a rural police force in the adjoining counties of Dunbarton, Renfrew and Stirling were made in 1838 on the grounds of weekly depredations on the part of city dwellers in their districts; in the previous year the fact that there was a 'large Manufacturing Population' in Dundee had persuaded the military authorities in Scotland that troops should be stationed there rather than Perth. The fear of dislocation and maintenance of social order, under which were subsumed hierarchy, morality and religion, became therefore the pressing issues for the authorities, more so even than the reform of the urban environment, although civic leaders did not overlook their responsibilities in this regard [86; 206].

While outbreaks of disorder continued to occur, it is arguable that the worst was over by 1850 and an uneasy peace had been established. The town in Scotland was to become 'a place of order' [217:*91*]. Indeed one historian has argued that by mid-century there had been a transformation amongst the Scottish working classes in which industrial violence, radicalism, Chartism and alternative visions of society gave way to 'a more harmonious and stable relationship between capital and labour based on a shared commitment to the values and ethos of liberal capitalism' [180:*218*]. Explaining this is not easy. It was the outcome of a complex set of factors which require further investigation. Arguably the most important of them is that after the intense industrial struggles of the 1820s and 1830s, decades during which trade union power had ebbed and flowed, Scottish capitalism appears to have been victorious and 'held the whip hand over a divided and unorganised working class' [271:*4*].

From the mid-1820s and outside the short periods of severe distress the numbers of working people who appear to have been willing to resort to violence were relatively small. Radicals in Scotland lacked anything like a substantial insurrectionary tradition [124:*73*]. The defeat of the cotton spinners' strike of 1837 by an alliance of state and cotton masters confirmed the trend [123:*162*]. Even during the desperate crisis of the early 1840s 'the working classes [in Paisley] identified with the propertied classes ... it was seen as a community and not a class problem', although it must be admitted that the prevalence of small manufacturers and marked sectionalism amongst the weavers, along with other factors, may make Paisley somewhat unusual [48]. By and large Scottish Chartism tended to be of the 'moral force' variety, with strong Christian and respectable impulses, its working-class adherents convinced of the benefits of self-improvement [124]. There were of course beneficiaries of industrialisation, the many thousands of pragmatic artisans – machine makers, millwrights and so on – who were prepared to eschew confrontation and needed little persuasion of the benefits of class collaboration and who formed over half of the membership of urban Presbyterian churches. A shortage of accommodation and the countrywide spread of pew-renting in the later eighteenth century (the 'intrusion of "free-market" economics into church life') had the effect of excluding the unskilled and lower-paid, as too did the need for decent clothing. Nevertheless, recent research has shown that contrary to long-established wisdom, in Scotland urban rates of church-going were higher than their hinterlands, with churches often acting as welcome anchors for the newcomers to urban society. This was not so immediate where Irish Catholics were concerned and whose allegiance had to be reclaimed once the shortfall in chapels and Irish-born priests in the urban areas began to be made up from the 1860s [217:*92*; 14:*20–1*]. Early provision was made for Gaelic-speaking Highlanders, with a Glasgow Highland Society being founded in 1727 for example and chapels being established in several towns such as Perth in 1781 and Dundee in 1791 [200]. Evangelical mission schemes in the early nineteenth century were directed at non-churchgoers with working-class revivalism being a widespread phenomenon in the smaller industrial communities in the 1830s and 1840s, particularly after episodes of economic distress [13:*323–4*].

Not to be overlooked either is the vigour of the urban authorities' response to fears of chaos and insurrection. Radicals and trouble-makers had been vigorously pursued and punished since the first appearance of Radicalism in the early 1790s. A network of government spies and informers ensured that anticipated risings were nipped in the bud [78]. Police forces were established which set about their task with considerable zeal. Moral crusading had its part to play too, as in the case of Glasgow's Sunday School movement, launched after the trauma of the weavers' strike of 1787. By 1819 they could boast a roll of 9,000, equivalent to 7 per cent of the city's population. In Scotland as a whole 567 schools were affiliated to the Sabbath School Union for Scotland [12:*158*]. Basic educational provision was also extended. The effect of the Industrial Revolution on the drinking habits of the working classes was 'dramatic' in Scotland, where drunkenness appears to have been more widespread than in England [99]. Whisky drinking in particular was commonplace from the 1790s and seen as a fundamental cause of poverty and a danger to morals, public order and productivity, thus generating in 1829 a powerful temperance movement in Scotland which was aimed at spirit drinking rather than beer. Although launched by middle-class men and of limited impact at first, its greatest appeal in the next two decades was to respectable members of the working class for whom temperance gatherings could have a messianic appeal [271:*141–2*]. Propaganda extolling the virtues of the capitalist way was fed into working-class consciousness through every available channel [123:*167*]. Nevertheless, while the assault on drink and disorder was having an effect, as too were employer attempts to create a more disciplined (and sober) workforce, what little investigation has been done on popular culture in Scotland suggests that 'boisterousness' continued well into the century while it was only after 1850 that consumption of drink began to fall, except perhaps in Greenock [125; 99].

There were still continuities in mid-nineteenth-century Scotland. The countryside was still important, though less so as either a place of residence or as a source of employment than it had been even in 1830. By the 1840s no Lowland county had a majority of its householders engaged in farming. The population of the rural counties peaked in 1831, falling unevenly thereafter. In 1851 however 25 per cent of the population still made its living from employment in the primary industries of agriculture, fishing and forestry. Despite the appearance near the top of the urban hierarchy of relatively new towns such as Paisley and Greenock (third and sixth respectively in 1801), the older regional centres continued to predominate, and can quite justifiably be considered as 'city regions', each dominated by 'urban centres so different that they defy generalisation' [217:*74*; 46]. If Paisley and Greenock and similar towns are categorised as satellites of the provincial capitals like Glasgow, the pattern of urban change was much less marked than in England: '[in Scotland] the regional centres of the sixteenth and seventeenth centuries became the industrial centres of the nineteenth' [310:*29*]. Within the workplace older rhythms could still be detected, and multiple occupations were still commonplace amongst rural tradesmen. In the fishing industry more and bigger boats were being used on the east coast but they were still open boats. The size of the herring catch increased but 'the organisation and social habits of the fishing villages altered to a surprisingly small extent' [137:*193*].

Substantial change therefore was still to come, but even so, Scotland had experienced revolutionary change over the hundred or so years which ended in 1850. Unmistakably it had become a new kind of society and an effective partner in the Workshop of the World.

References

Abbreviations

EHR Economic History Review
JEH Journal of Economic History
JSLHS Journal of the Scottish Labour History Society
NS Northern Scotland
SGM Scottish Geographical Magazine
SHR Scottish Historical Review
SESH Scottish Economic & Social History

1. Adams, I. H. (1978) *The Making of Urban Scotland* (London).
2. Adams, I. H. (1980) 'The Agents of Agricultural Change' in [233].
3. Allan, D. (1993) *Virtue, Learning and the Scottish Enlightenment* (Edinburgh).
4. Behagg, C. (1988) 'The Democracy of Work, 1820–1850' in [249].
5. Bennett, H. (1987) 'The Shetland Handknitting Industry' in [20].
6. Berg, M. and P. Hudson (1992) 'Rehabilitating the Industrial Revolution', *EHR*, 45, 1.
7. Berg, M. (1993) 'What Difference did Women's Work Make to the Industrial Revolution?', *History Workshop Journal*, 35.
8. Berg, M. (1994 edn) *The Age of Manufactures 1700–1820: Industry, Innovation and Work in Britain* (London and New York).
9. Bolin-Hort, P. (1989) *Work, State and Family: Child Labour and the Organisation of Production in the British Cotton Industry, 1780–1920* (Lund).
10. Bolin-Hort, P. (1994) 'Managerial Strategies and Worker Responses: A New Perspective on the Decline of the Scottish Cotton Industry', *JSLHS*, 29.
11. Brotherstone, T. (ed.) (1989) *Covenant, Charter and Party: Traditions of Revolt and Protest in Modern Scottish History* (Aberdeen).
12. Brown, C. G. (1988) 'Religion and Social Change' in [92].
13. Brown, C. G. (1990) 'Religion, Class and Church Growth' in [126].
14. Brown, C. G. (1993) *The People in the Pews* (Glasgow).
15. Butt, J. (1966) 'The Scottish Iron and Steel Industry Before the Hot-Blast', *Jnl. of the West of Scotland Iron and Steel Institute*, 73.
16. Butt, J. (1967) *The Industrial Archaeology of Scotland* (Newton Abbot).

17. Butt, J. (1976) 'Capital and Enterprise in the Scottish Iron Industry 1780–1840' in [21].
18. Butt, J. (1977) 'The Scottish Cotton Industry During the Industrial Revolution, 1780–1840' in [61].
19. Butt, J. (1987) 'Labour and Industrial Relations in the Scottish Cotton Industry During the Industrial Revolution' in [20].
20. Butt, J. and K.Ponting (eds.) (1987) *Scottish Textile History* (Aberdeen).
21. Butt, J. and J. T. Ward (eds.) (1976) *Scottish Themes* (Edinburgh).
22. Cage, R. A. (1983) 'The Standard of Living Debate: Glasgow, 1800–1850', *JEH*, 43, 1.
23. Cage, R. A. (1985) 'The Scots in England' in [24].
24. Cage, R. A. (ed.) (1985) *The Scots Abroad: Labour, Capital and Enterprise, 1750–1914* (London).
25. Cameron, R. (1982) 'Banking and Industrialisation in Britain in the Nineteenth Century' in [259].
26. Cameron, R. (1994) 'The Industrial Revolution: Fact or Fiction?', *Contention*, 4, 1.
27. Campbell, A. B. (1979) *The Lanarkshire Miners: A Social History of their Trade Unions, 1775–1874* (Edinburgh).
28. Campbell, A. B. (1988) 'The Scots Colliers' Strikes of 1824–1826: the Years of Freedom and Independence' in [249].
29. Campbell, R. H. (1961) *Carron Company* (Edinburgh and London).
30. Campbell, R. H. (1965) *Scotland Since 1707* (Oxford).
31. Campbell, R. H. (1967) 'The Industrial Revolution: a Revision Article', *SHR*, 46, 1.
32. Campbell, R. H. (ed.) (1978) *Scottish Industrial History: A Miscellany* (Edinburgh).
33. Campbell, R. H. (1980) *The Rise and Fall of Scottish Industry 1707–1939* (Edinburgh).
34. Campbell, R. H. (1982) 'The Enlightenment and the Economy' in [40].
35. Campbell, R. H. (1983a) 'The Influence of Religion on Economic Growth in Scotland in the Eighteenth Century' in [90].
36. Campbell, R. H. (1983b) 'Agricultural Labour in the South-West' in [73].
37. Campbell, R. H. (1988) 'The Landed Classes' in [92].
38. Campbell, R. H. (1995) 'The Making of the Industrial City' in [91].
39. Campbell, R. H. and T. M. Devine (1990) 'The Rural Experience' in [126].
40. Campbell, R. H. and A. Skinner (eds.) (1982) *The Origins and Nature of the Scottish Enlightenment* (Edinburgh).
41. Carter, J. and J. H. Pittock (eds.) (1987) *Aberdeen and the Enlightenment* (Aberdeen).
42. Chapman. S. D. (1987 edn) *The Cotton Industry in the Industrial Revolution* (London).
43. Chapman, S. D. and J. Butt (1988) 'The Cotton Industry 1775–1850' in [117].
44. Chartres, J. A. (ed.) (1994) *Pre-industrial Britain* (Oxford).
45. Checkland, S. G. (1975) *Scottish Banking: A History, 1695–1973* (Glasgow and London).
46. Checkland, S. G. and O. (1984) *Industry and Ethos: Scotland 1832–1914* (London).

47. Chitnis, A. C. (1982) 'Provost Drummond and the Origins of Edinburgh Medicine' in [40].
48. Clarke, T. and T. Dickson, (1982) 'Class and Class Consciousness in Early Industrial Capitalism: Paisley 1770–1850' in [95].
49. Cochran, L. E. (1985) *Scottish Trade with Ireland in the Eighteenth Century* (Edinburgh).
50. Collins, B. (1988) 'Sewing and Social Structure: The Flowerers of Scotland and Ireland' in [214].
51. Collins, B. (1991) 'The Origins of Irish Immigration to Scotland in the Nineteenth and Twentieth Centuries' in [80].
52. Cooke, A. J. (1995) 'Cotton and the Scottish Highland Clearances – the Development of Spinningdale 1791–1806', *Textile History*, 26, 1.
53. Cottrell, P. and D. H. Aldcroft (eds.) (1981) *Shipping, Trade and Commerce* (Leicester).
54. Coull, J. R. (1989) 'Fishing and Fishing Settlements of the Grampian Region' in [262].
55. Crafts, N. F. R. (1985) *British Economic Growth During the Industrial Revolution* (Oxford).
56. Crawford, W. H. (1983) 'Ulster as a Mirror of the Two Societies' in [90].
57. Cregeen, E. (1970) 'The Changing Role of the House of Argyll in the Scottish Highlands' in [236].
58. Cullen, L. M. (1977) 'Merchant Communities Overseas, the Navigation Acts and Irish and Scottish Responses' in [61].
59. Cullen, L. M. (1983) 'Incomes, Social Classes and Economic Growth in Ireland and Scotland, 1600–1900' in [90].
60. Cullen, L. M. (1989) 'Scotland and Ireland, 1600–1800: Their Role in the Evolution of British Society' in [161].
61. Cullen, L. M. and T. C. Smout (eds.) (1977) *Comparative Aspects of Scottish & Irish Economic and Social History* (Edinburgh).
62. Cullen, L. M., T. C. Smout and A. Gibson (1988) 'Wages and Comparative Development in Ireland and Scotland, 1565–1780' in [213].
63. Cummings, A. J. G. (1994) 'Industry and Investment in the Eighteenth Century Highlands: the York Buildings Company of London' in [64].
64. Cummings, A. J. G. and T. M. Devine (eds.) (1994) *Industry, Business and Society in Scotland Since 1700* (Edinburgh).
65. Daunton, M. J. (1995) *Progress and Poverty* (Oxford).
66. Davis, R. (1979) *The Industrial Revolution and British Overseas Trade* (Leicester).
67. Deane, P. and W. A. Cole (1962) *British Economic Growth, 1688–1959* (Cambridge).
68. Devine, T. M. (1975) *The Tobacco Lords* (Edinburgh).
69. Devine, T. M. (1982) 'The Scottish Merchant Community, 1680–1740' in [40].
70. Devine, T. M. (1983a) 'The English Connection and Irish and Scottish Development in the Eighteenth Century' in [90].
71. Devine, T. M. (1983b) 'Introduction: Scottish Farm Service in the Agricultural Revolution' in [73].
72. Devine, T. M. (1983c) 'Women Workers, 1850–1914' in [73].
73. Devine, T. M. (ed.) (1983d) *Farm Servants and Labour in Lowland Scotland 1770–1914* (Edinburgh).

74. Devine, T. M. (1985) 'The Union of 1707 and Scottish Development', *SESH*, 5.
75. Devine, T. M. (1988a) 'Urbanisation' in [92].
76. Devine, T. M. (1988b) *The Great Highland Famine* (Edinburgh).
77. Devine, T. M. (ed.) (1990a) *Conflict and Stability in Scottish Society, 1700–1850* (Edinburgh).
78. Devine, T. M. (1990b) 'The Failure of Radical Reform in Scotland in the Late Eighteenth Century: the Social and Economic Context' in [77].
79. Devine, T. M. (1991a) 'Introduction' in [80].
80. Devine, T. M. (ed.) (1991b) *Irish Immigration and Scottish Society* (Edinburgh).
81. Devine. T. M. (1991b) 'The Making of Industrial and Urban Society: Scotland 1780–1840' in [213].
82. Devine, T. M. (1994a) *The Transformation of Rural Scotland* (Edinburgh).
83. Devine, T. M. (1994b) (ed.) *Scottish Elites* (Edinburgh).
84. Devine, T. M. (1994c) *Clanship to Crofters War* (Manchester).
85. Devine, T. M. (1994d) 'The Making of a Farming Elite? Lowland Scotland, 1750–1850' in [83].
86. Devine, T. M. (1994e) 'Urbanisation and the Civic Response: Glasgow 1800–1830' in [64].
87. Devine, T. M. (1995a) 'Introduction: The Development of Glasgow to 1830: Medieval Burgh to Industrial City' in [91].
88. Devine, T. M. (1995b) 'The Golden Age of Tobacco' in [91].
89. Devine, T. M. (1995c) 'The Urban Crisis' in [91].
90. Devine, T. M. and D. Dickson (eds.) (1983) *Ireland and Scotland 1600–1850: Parallels and Contrasts in Economic and Social Development* (Edinburgh).
91. Devine, T. M. and G. Jackson (eds.) (1995) *Glasgow Volume I: Beginnings to 1830* (Manchester).
92. Devine, T. M. and R. Mitchison (eds.) (1988) *People and Society in Scotland, Volume I, 1760–1830* (Edinburgh).
93. Dickson, D. (1977) 'Aspects of the Rise and Decline of the Irish Cotton Industry' in [61].
94. Dickson, T. (ed.) (1980) *Scottish Capitalism* (London).
95. Dickson, T. (ed.) (1982) *Capital and Class in Scotland* (Edinburgh).
96. Dingwall, H. (1994) *Late Seventeenth-Century Edinburgh* (Aldershot).
97. Dodgshon, R. A. (1981) *Land and Society in early Scotland* (Oxford).
98. Donnachie, I. (1979a) *A History of the Brewing Industry in Scotland* (Edinburgh).
99. Donnachie, I. (1979b) 'Drink and Society 1750–1850: Some Aspects of the Scottish Experience', *JSLHS*, 13.
100. Donnachie, I (1987) 'The Textile Industry in South West Scotland 1750–1914' in [20].
101. Donnachie, I. (1992) 'The Enterprising Scot' in [105].
102. Donnachie, I. (1994) 'A Tour of the Works: Early Scottish Industry Observed, 1790–1825' in [64].
103. Donnachie, I. (1995) ' "The Darker Side": A Speculative Survey of Scottish Crime During the First Half of the Nineteenth Century', *SESH*, 15.
104. Donnachie, I. and G. Hewitt (1993) *Historic New Lanark* (Edinburgh).

105. Donnachie, I and C. A. Whatley (eds.) (1992) *The Manufacture of Scottish History* (Edinburgh).
106. Donnelly, T. (1981) 'Shipbuilding in Aberdeen, 1750–1914', *NS*, 4.
107. Donnelly, T. (1994) 'Tombstone Territory: Granite Manufacturing in Aberdeen, 1830–1914' in [64].
108. Duckham, B. F. (1970) *A History of the Scottish Coal Industry 1700–1815* (Newton Abbot).
109. Duckham, B. F. (1976) 'English Influences in the Scottish Coal Industry 1700–1815' in [21].
110. Durie, A. J. (1973) 'The Markets for Scottish Linen, 1730–1775', *SHR*, 52, 1.
111. Durie, A. J. (1979) *The Scottish Linen Industry in the Eighteenth Century* (Edinburgh).
112. Durie, A. J. (1984) 'Balanced and Unbalanced Urban Economies: Aberdeen and Dundee, 1800–1914', *Scotia*, 8.
113. Durie, A. J. (1987) 'Textile Finishing in the North East of Scotland 1727–1860' in [20].
114. Durie, A. J. (1991) 'Market Forces or Government Intervention: The Spectacular Growth of the Linen Industry in Eighteenth Century Scotland', *Scotia*, 15.
115. Durie, A, J. and P. Solar (1988) 'The Scottish and Irish Linen Industries Compared, 1780–1860' in [214].
116. Emerson, R. (1995) 'Scottish Cultural Change 1660–1710 and the Union of 1707' in [246].
117. Feinstein, C. H. and S. Pollard (eds.) (1988) *Studies in Capital Formation in the United Kingdom 1750–1920* (Oxford).
118. Fitton, R. S. (1989) *The Arkwrights: Spinners of Fortune* (Manchester).
119. Flinn, M. W. *et al.* (1977) *Scottish Population History from the Seventeenth Century to the 1930s* (Cambridge).
120. Flinn, M. W. (1984) *The History of the British Coal Industry Volume II, 1700–1830: The Industrial Revolution* (Oxford).
121. Fraser, W. H. (1976) 'The Glasgow Cotton Spinners, 1837' in [21].
122. Fraser, W. H. (1988a) 'Patterns of Protest' in [92].
123. Fraser, W. H. (1988b) *Conflict and Class* (Edinburgh).
124. Fraser, W. H. (1989) 'The Scottish Context of Chartism' in [11].
125. Fraser, W. H. (1990) 'Developments in Leisure' in [126].
126. Fraser, W. H. and R. J. Morris (eds.) (1990) *People and Society in Scotland, Volume II, 1830–1914* (Edinburgh)
127. Fry, M. (1992) *The Dundas Despotism* (Edinburgh).
128. Gauldie, E. (1969) *The Dundee Textile Industry, 1790–1885* (Edinburgh).
129. Gauldie, E. (1987) 'The Dundee Jute Industry' in [20].
130. Gibson, A. J. S. and T. C. Smout (1989) 'Scottish Food and Scottish History, 1500–1800' in [161].
131. Gibson, A. J. S. and T. C. Smout (1995a) *Prices, Food and Wages in Scotland, 1550–1780* (Cambridge).
132. Gibson, A. J. S. and T. C. Smout (1995b) 'Regional Prices and Market Regions: the Evolution of the Early Modern Scottish Grain Market', *EHR*, 48, 2.
133. Gordon, E. (1991) *Women and the Labour Movement in Scotland 1850–1914* (Oxford).
134. Gordon, G. (ed.) (1986) *Perspectives of the Scottish City* (Aberdeen).

135. Gourvish, T. R. (1972) 'The Cost of Living in Glasgow in the Early Nineteenth Century', *EHR*, 25, 1.
136. Gray, M. (1957) *The Highland Economy* (Edinburgh).
137. Gray, M. (1967) 'Organisation and Growth in the East Coast Herring Fishing, 1800–1885' in [234].
138. Gray, M. (1988) 'The Social Impact of Agrarian Change in the Rural Lowlands' in [92].
139. Gray, M. (1990) *Scots on the Move: Scots Migrants 1750–1914* (Glasgow).
140. Gulvin, C. (1973) *The Tweedmakers* (Newton Abbot).
141. Gulvin, C. (1984) *The Scottish Hosiery and Knitwear Industry, 1680–1980* (Edinburgh).
142. Guy, I. (1986) 'The Scottish Export Trade, 1460–1599' in [272].
143. Hamilton, H. (1932, 1966 edn) *The Industrial Revolution in Scotland* (Oxford).
144. Hamilton, H. (1963) *An Economic History of Scotland in the Eighteenth Century* (Oxford).
145. Harley, C. K. (1982) 'British Industrialisation Before 1841: Evidence of Slower Growth During the Industrial Revolution', *JEH*, 42.
146. Harvie, C. (1993) 'Scottish Industrialisation, *c.*1750–1880' in [251].
147. Hassan, J. A. (1980) 'The Landed Estate, Paternalism and the Coal Industry in Midlothian, 1800–80', *SHR*, 59.
148. Hatcher, J. (1993) *The History of the British Coal Industry, Volume I: Before 1700* (Oxford).
149. Hont, I. (1983) 'The "Rich Country-Poor Country" Debate in Scottish Classical Political Economy' in [150].
150. Hont, I. and M. Ignatieff (eds.) (1983) *Wealth and Virtue* (Cambridge).
151. Hook, A. and R. Sher (eds.) (1995) *The Glasgow Enlightenment* (East Linton).
152. Hoppit, J. (1987) 'Understanding the Industrial Revolution', *Historical Journal*, 30, 1.
153. Hoppit, J. (1990) 'Counting the Industrial Revolution', *EHR*, 43, 2.
154. Hoppit, J. and E. A. Wrigley (eds.) (1994) *The Industrial Revolution in Britain* (London).
155. Houston, G. (1958) 'Labour Relations in Scottish Agriculture before 1870', *Agricultural History Review*, 6.
156. Houston, R. A. (1983) 'Coal, Class and Culture: Labour Relations in a Scottish Mining Community, 1650–1750', *Social History*, 8.
157. Houston, R. A. (1985) *Scottish Literacy and Scottish Identity* (Cambridge).
158. Houston, R. A. (1988) 'The Demographic Regime' in [92].
159. Houston, R. A. (1989) 'Women in the Economy and Society of Scotland, 1500–1800' in [161].
160. Houston, R. A. (1994) *Social Change in the Age of the Enlightenment: Edinburgh, 1660–1760* (Oxford).
161. Houston, R. A. and I. D. Whyte (eds.) (1989) *Scottish Society 1500–1800* (Cambridge).
162. Houston, R. A. and C. W. J. Withers (1990) 'Population Mobility in Scotland and Europe, 1600–1900: A Comparative Perspective', *Annales De Demographie Historique* (Paris).
163. Hudson, P. (ed.) (1989) *Regions and Industries: A Perspective on the Industrial Revolution in Britain* (Cambridge).
164. Hume, J. R. (1980) *Early Days in a Dundee Mill 1819–1823* (Dundee).

165. Hunt, E. H. (1973) *Regional Wage Variations in Britain 1850–1914* (Oxford).
166. Hunt, E. H. (1986) 'Industrialisation and Regional Inequality: Wages in Britain, 1760–1914', *JEH*, 46, 4.
167. Hunter, J. (1976) *The Making of the Crofting Community* (Edinburgh).
168. Hyde, C. K. (1977) *Technological Change and the British Iron Industry, 1700–1870* (New Jersey).
169. Jackson, G. (1976) 'Government Bounties and the Establishment of the Scottish Whaling Trade, 1750–1800' in [21].
170. Jackson, G. (1981) 'Scottish Shipping, 1775–1805' in [53].
171. Jackson, G. (1986) 'Sea Trade' in [182].
172. Jackson, G. (1995a) 'Glasgow in Transition, c.1660–c.1740' in [91].
173. Jackson, G. (1995b) 'New Horizons in Trade' in [91].
174. Jackson G. and K. Kinnear (1991) *The Trade and Shipping of Dundee 1780–1850* (Dundee).
175. Jackson, R. V. (1992) 'Rates of Industrial Growth During the Industrial Revolution', *EHR*, 45, I.
176. Jenkins, D. T. (1988) 'The Wool Textile Industry 1780–1850' in [117].
177. Jenkins, D. T. and K. G. Ponting (1982) *The British Wool Textile Industry 1770–1914* (London).
178. Kendrick, S., D. McCrone and F. Bechhofer (1984) 'Industrial and Occupational Structure' (Working Paper 2, Social Structure of Modern Scotland Project, University of Edinburgh).
179. Knox, W. W. (1990) 'The Political and Workplace Culture of the Scottish Working Class, 1832–1914' in [126].
180. Knox, W. W. (1992) 'Whatever Happened to Radical Scotland?' in [204].
181. Knox, W. W. (1995) *Hanging By a Thread: The Scottish Cotton Industry, c.1850–1914* (Preston).
182. Langton, J. and R. J. Morris (eds.) *Atlas of Industrialising Britain, 1780–1914* (London).
183. Larner, C. (1983 edn) *Enemies of God* (Oxford).
184. Lee, C. H. (1979) *British Regional Employment Statistics, 1841–1971* (Cambridge).
185. Lee, C. H. (1983) 'Modern Economic Growth and Structural Change in Scotland: The Service Sector Reconsidered', *SESH*, 3.
186. Leneman, L. (1986) *Living in Atholl 1685–1785* (Edinburgh).
187. Leneman, L. (ed.) (1988) *Perspectives in Scottish Social History* (Edinburgh).
188. Lenman, B. (1976) *From Esk to Tweed* (Glasgow).
189. Lenman, B. (1977) *An Economic History of Modern Scotland* (London).
190. Lenman, B. (1981) *Integration, Enlightenment and Industrialisation: Scotland 1746–1832* (London).
191. Lenman, B., C. Lythe and E. Gauldie (1969) *Dundee and its Textile Industry* (Dundee).
192. Levitt, I. and T. C. Smout (1979) *The State of the Scottish Working Class in 1843* (Edinburgh).
193. Lindsay, J. M. (1977) 'The Iron Industry in the Highlands', *SHR*, 56, 1.
194. Linebaugh, P. (1991) *The London Hanged: Crime and Civil Society in the Eighteenth Century* (London).
195. Lochrie, M. (1997) 'The Paisley Shawl Industry' in [20].

196. Lockhart, D. G. (1983) 'Planned Village Development in Scotland and Ireland, 1700–1850' in [90].
197. Lynch, M. (ed.) (1987) *The Early Modern Town in Scotland* (London).
198. Lynch, M. (1992) 'Urbanisation and Urban Networks in Seventeenth Century Scotland', *SESH*, 12.
199. Lythe, S. G. E. and J. Butt (1976) *An Economic History of Scotland* (Glasgow).
200. Macdonald, I. R. (1995) *Glasgow's Gaelic Churches: Highland Religion in an Urban Setting 1690–1995* (Edinburgh).
201. Macinnes, A. I. (1988) 'Scottish Gaeldom: The First Phase of Clearance' in [92].
202. Macinnes, A. I. (1994) 'Landownership, Land Use and Elite Enterprise in Scottish Gaeldom: From Clanship to Clearance in Argyllshire, 1688–1858' in [83].
203. Marshall, G. (1980) *Presbyteries and Profits: Calvinism and the Development of Capitalism in Scotland, 1560–1707* (Edinburgh).
204. Mason, R. and N. Macdougall (eds.) (1992) *People and Power in Scotland* (Edinburgh).
205. Mathias, P. (1983 edn) *The First Industrial Nation* (London).
206. Maver, I. (1995) 'The Guardianship of the Community: Civic Authority before 1833' in [91].
207. McFarland, E. (1990) *Protestants First* (Edinburgh).
208. Michie, R. C. (1977–78) 'North-east Scotland and the Northern Whale Fishing, 1752–1983', *NS*, 3, 1.
209. Mitchell, B. R. and P. Deane (1962) *Abstract of British Historical Statistics* (Cambridge).
210. Mitchison, R. (1978) *Life in Scotland* (London).
211. Mitchison, R. (1983) 'Ireland and Scotland: The Seventeenth-Century Legacies Compared' in [90].
212. Mitchison, R. (1988) 'The Poor Law' in [92].
213. Mitchison, R. (ed.) (1991) *Why Scottish History Matters* (Edinburgh).
214. Mitchison, R. and P. Roebuck (eds.) (1988) *Economy and Society in Scotland and Ireland 1500–1939* (Edinburgh).
215. Mokyr, J. (1985) *Why Ireland Starved: A Quantitative and Analytical History of the Irish Economy, 1800–1850* (London).
216. Mokyr, J. (ed.) (1992) *The British Industrial Revolution* (Colorado).
217. Morris, R. J. (1990) 'Urbanisation and Scotland' in [126].
218. Moss, M. and J. R. Hume (1977) *Workshop of the British Empire: Engineering and Shipbuilding in the West of Scotland* (London).
219. Moss, M. and J. R. Hume (1981) *A History of the Scottish Whisky Industry* (Edinburgh).
220. Munn, C. W. (1981) *The Scottish Provincial Banking Companies 1747–1864* (Edinburgh).
221. Munro, J. (1989) 'The Planned Villages of the British Fisheries Society' in [262].
222. Murray, N. (1978) *The Scottish Hand Loom Weavers, 1790–1850* (Edinburgh).
223. Murray, N. (1994) 'The Regional Structure of Textile Employment in Scotland in the Nineteenth Century: East of Scotland Textile Weavers in the 1830s' in [64].

224. Nenadic, S. (1988) 'The Rise of the Urban Middle Class' in [92].
225. Nenadic, S. (1995) 'The Middle Ranks and Modernisation' in [91].
226. O'Brien, P. K. (1993a) 'Modern Conceptions of the Industrial Revolution' in [228].
227. O'Brien, P. K. (1993b), 'Political Preconditions for the Industrial Revolution', in [228].
228. O'Brien, P. K. and R. Quinault (eds.) (1993) *The Industrial Revolution and British Society* (Cambridge).
229. O'Brien, P. K., G. Griffiths and P. Hunt (1991), 'Political Components of the Industrial Revolution: Parliament and the English Cotton Textile Industry, 1660–1774', *EHR*, 44, 3.
230. O'Grada, C. (1988) *Ireland Before and After the Famine* (Manchester).
231. Parker, G. (1988) 'The "Kirk By Law Established" and the Origins of "The Taming of Scotland": St Andrews 1559–1600' in [187].
232. Parker, J. G. (1985) 'Scottish Enterprise in India 1750–1914' in [24].
233. Parry, M. L. and T. R. Slater (eds.) (1980) *The Making of the Scottish Countryside* (London).
234. Payne, P. L. (ed.) (1967) *Studies in Scottish Business History* (London).
235. Payne, P. L. (1974) *British Entrepreneurship in the Nineteenth Century* (London).
236. Phillipson, N. T. and R. Mitchison (eds.) (1970) *Scotland in the Age of Improvement* (Edinburgh).
237. Pollard, S. (1965) *The Genesis of Modern Management* (London).
238. Pollard, S. (1980) 'A New Estimate of British Coal production 1750–1850', *EHR*, 33, 2.
239. Pollard, S. (1981) *Peaceful Conquest: The Industrialisation of Europe, 1760–1970* (Oxford).
240. Ponting, K. (1987) 'The Scottish Contribution to Wool Textile Design in the Nineteenth Century' in [20].
241. Price, J. M. (1984) 'Glasgow, the Tobacco Trade, and the Scottish Customs, 1707–1730', *SHR*, 63, 1.
242. Richards E. (1973) *The Leviathan of Wealth: The Sutherland Fortune in the Industrial Revolution* (London).
243. Richards, E. (1982) *A History of the Highland Clearances* (London).
244. Richards, E. (1993) 'Margins of the Industrial Revolution' in [228].
245. Robertson, C. J. A. (1983) *The Origins of the Scottish Railway System 1722–1844* (Edinburgh).
246. Robertson, J. (ed.) (1995) *A Union for Empire: Political Thought and the Union of 1707* (Cambridge).
247. Rodger, R. (1985) 'Employment, Wages and Poverty in the Scottish Cities 1841–1914' in [134].
248. Roebuck, P. (1988) 'The Economic Situation and Functions of Substantial Landowners, 1660–1815: Ulster and Lowland Scotland Compared' in [214].
249. Rule, J. (1988) *British Trade Unionism, 1750–1850: The Formative Years* (London).
250. Samuel, R. (1977) 'Workshop of the World: Steam Power and Hand Technology in mid-Victorian Britain', *History Workshop*, 3.
251. Schulze, R. (ed.) (1993) *Industrial Regions in Transformation* (Essen).
252. Shaw, F. (1980) *The Northern and Western Islands of Scotland* (Edinburgh).

253. Shaw, J. (1984) *Water Power in Scotland 1550–1870* (Edinburgh).
254. Shaw, J. S. (1983) *The Management of Scottish Society, 1707–1764* (Edinburgh).
255. Sher, R. (1995) 'Commerce, Religion and The Enlightenment in Eighteenth-Century Glasgow' in [91].
256. Simpson, G. G. (ed.) (1990) *Scotland and Scandinavia, 800–1800* (Edinburgh).
257. Skinner, B. C. (1969) *The Lime Industry in the Lothians* (Edinburgh).
258. Slaven, A. (1976) *The Development of the West of Scotland 1750–1960* (London).
259. Slaven, A. and D. H. Aldcroft (1982) *Business, Banking and Urban History: Essays in Honour of S. G. Checkland* (Edinburgh).
260. Sloan, W. (1994) 'Employment Opportunities and Migrant Group Assimilation: the Highlanders and Irish in Glasgow, 1840–1860' in [64].
261. Smith, J. S. and D. Stevenson (eds.) (1988) *Aberdeen in the Nineteenth Century* (Aberdeen).
262. Smith, J. S. and D. Stevenson (eds.) (1989) *Farmfolk and Fisherfolk: Rural Life in Northern Scotland in the Eighteenth and Nineteenth Centuries* (Aberdeen).
263. Smout, T. C. (1963) *Scottish Trade on the Eve of the Union* (Edinburgh).
264. Smout, T. C. (1964) 'Scottish Landowners and Economic Growth, 1650–1850', *Scottish Journal of Political Economy*, 11.
265. Smout, T. C. (1967) 'Lead-mining in Scotland, 1650–1850' in [234].
266. Smout, T. C. (1969, 1981 edn) *A History of the Scottish People 1560–1830* (London).
267. Smout, T. C. (1970) 'The Landowner and the Planned Village in Scotland, 1730–1830' in [236].
268. Smout, T. C. (1980a) 'Scotland and England: Is Dependency a Symptom or a Cause of Underdevelopment ?', *Review*, 3, 4.
269. Smout, T. C. (1980b) 'Centre and Periphery in History; With Some Thoughts on Scotland as a Case Study', *Jnl. of Common Market Studies*, 18, 3.
270. Smout, T. C. (1983) 'Where had the Scottish Economy Got to by the Third Quarter of the Eighteenth Century' in [150].
271. Smout, T. C. (1986a) *A Century of the Scottish People, 1830–1950* (London).
272. Smout, T. C. (ed.) (1986b) *Scotland and Europe* (Edinburgh).
273. Smout, T. C. (1987) 'Landowners in Scotland, Ireland and Denmark in the Age of Improvement', *Scandinavian Journal of History*, 12.
274. Soltow, L. (1990) 'The Distribution of Private Wealth in Land in Scotland and Scandinavia in the Seventeenth and Eighteenth Centuries' in [256].
275. Stevenson, D. (ed.) (1986) *From Lairds to Louns* (Aberdeen).
276. Stevenson, D. (1991) 'Twilight before Night or Darkness before Dawn? Interpreting Seventeenth-Century Scotland' in [213].
277. Sylla, R. and G. Toniolo (eds.) (1991) *Patterns of European Industrialisation* (London).
278. Tarrant, N. (1987) 'The Turkey Red Dyeing Industry in the Vale of Leven' in [20].
279. Thomson, A. G. (1974) *The Paper Industry in Scotland, 1590–1861* (Edinburgh).

280. Thomson, W. P. L. (1983) *Kelp-Making in Orkney* (Kirkwall).
281. Trainor, R. H. and N. Morgan (1990) 'The Dominant Classes' in [126].
282. Treble, J. T. (1988) 'The Standard of Living of the Working Class in [92].
283. Turner, W. H. K. (1982) 'The Development of Flax-Spinning Mills in Scotland 1787–1840', *SGM*, 98, 1.
284. Turner, W. H. K. (1983) 'Flax Weaving in Scotland in the Early 19th Century', *SGM*, 99, 1.
285. Tyson, R. E. (1986) 'Famine in Aberdeenshire, 1695–1699: Anatomy of a Crisis' in [275].
286. Tyson, R. E. (1988) 'The Economy of Aberdeen' in [261].
287. Tyson, R. E. (1989) 'The Rise and Fall of Manufacturing in Rural Aberdeenshire' in [262].
288. Vamplew, W. (1971) 'Railways and the Transformation of the Scottish Economy', *EHR*, 24, I.
289. Walker, G. (1991) 'The Protestant Irish in Scotland' in [80].
290. Wallerstein, I. (1980) 'One man's Meat: the Great Scottish Leap Forward', *Review*, 3, 4.
291. Watson, M. (1990) *Jute and Flax Mills in Dundee* (Tayport).
292. Weatherill, L. M. (1982) 'Marketing English Pottery in Scotland, 1750–1820: A Study in the Inland Trade', *SESH*, 2.
293. Weatherill, L. M. (1988) *Consumer Behaviour and Material Culture in Britain 1660–1760* (London).
294. Whatley, C. A. (1983) 'The Finest Place for a Lasting Colliery: Coal Mining Enterprise in Ayrshire *c.*1600–1840', *Ayrshire Collections*, 14, 2.
295. Whatley, C. A. (1987) *The Scottish Salt Industry, c.1570–1850: An Economic and Social History* (Aberdeen).
296. Whatley, C. A. (1988) 'The Experience of Work' in [92].
297. Whatley, C. A. (1989) 'Economic Causes and Consequences of the Union of 1707: A Survey', *SHR*, 68, 2.
298. Whatley, C. A. (1990) 'How Tame Were the Scottish Lowlanders During the Eighteenth Century?' in [77].
299. Whatley, C. A. (1992a) *The Remaking of Juteopolis: Dundee c.1891–1991* (Dundee).
300. Whatley, C. A. (1992b) 'The Making of "Juteopolis" - and How It Was' in [299].
301. Whatley, C. A. (1992c) *Onwards from Osnaburgs: The Rise and Progress of a Scottish Textile Firm: Don & Low of Forfar, c.1792–1992* (Edinburgh).
302. Whatley, C. A. (1992d) 'An Uninflammable People?' in [105].
303. Whatley, C. A. (1994a) 'New Light on Nef's Numbers: Coal Mining and the First Phase of Scottish Industrialisation, *c.*1700–1830' in [64].
304. Whatley, C. A. (1994b) 'Women and the Economic Transformation of Scotland, *c.*1740–1830', *SESH*, 14.
305. Whatley, C. A. (1995) 'Labour in the Industrialising City, 1660–1830' in [91].
306. Whittington, G. and I. D. Whyte (eds.) (1983) *An Historical Geography of Scotland* (London).
307. Whyte, I. (1979) *Agriculture and Society in Seventeenth Century Scotland* (Edinburgh).
308. Whyte, I. D. (1983) 'Early Modern Scotland: Continuity and Change' in [306].

309. Whyte, I. D. (1987) 'The Occupational Structure of the Scottish Burghs in the Late Seventeenth Century' in [197].

310. Whyte, I. D. (1989a) 'Urbanisation in Early-Modern Scotland', *SESH*, 9.

311. Whyte, I. D. (1989b) 'Proto-industrialisation in Scotland' in [163].

312. Whyte, I. D. (1989c) 'Population Mobility in Early Modern Scotland' in [161].

313. Whyte, I D. and K. Whyte (1983) 'Some Aspects of the Structure of Rural Society in Seventeenth-Century Lowland Scotland' in [90].

314. Whyte, I. D. and K. Whyte (1988) 'Debt and Credit, Poverty and Prosperity in a Seventeenth-Century Scottish Rural Community' in [214].

315. Withers, C. W. J. (1986) *Highland Communities in Dundee and Perth, 1787–1891* (Dundee).

316. Withrington, D. J. (1987) 'What was Distinctive about the Scottish Enlightenment?' in [41].

317. Woodward, D. (1977) 'A Comparative Study of the Irish and Scottish Livestock Trades in the Seventeenth Century' in [61].

318. Wrightson, K. (1989) 'Kindred adjoining Kingdoms: an English Perspective on the Social and Economic History of Early Modern Scotland' in [161].

319. Wrigley, E. A. (1988; 1993 edn) *Continuity, Chance and Change: The Character of the Industrial Revolution in England* (Cambridge).

320. Young, C. (1994) 'The Economic Characteristics of Small Craft Businesses in Rural Lowland Perthshire', *Business History*, 36.

321. Young, C. (1996) 'Rural Independent Artisan Production in the East-Central Lowlands of Scotland, *c*.1660–*c*.1850', *SESH*, 16.

Index

New Studies in Economic and Social History

Titles in the series available from Cambridge University Press:

Previously published as

Studies in Economic and Social History

Titles in the series available from the Macmillan Press Limited:

Economic History Society

The Economic History Society, which numbers around 3,000 members, publishes the *Economic History Review* four times a year (free to members) and holds an annual conference.

Enquiries about membership should be addressed to

The Assistant Secretary
Economic History Society
PO Box 70
Kingswood
Bristol
BS15 5TB

Full time students may join at special rates.

DATE DUE

NOV 0 5 1998			
	DEC 2 1 1998		
MAR 0 1 2001			
			Printed in USA

HIGHSMITH #45230